The Bakers' Manual
FOR QUANTITY BAKING
AND PASTRY MAKING

This book is to be returned on or before the last date stamped below.

Withdrawn

The Bakers' Manual

FOR QUANTITY BAKING
AND PASTRY MAKING

Revised Third Edition

JOSEPH AMENDOLA

The Culinary Institute of America, Inc.

 VAN NOSTRAND REINHOLD
New York

This book is dedicated to my wife,
Marjorie D. Amendola

Van Nostrand Reinhold
115 Fifth Avenue
New York, New York 10003

Chapman and Hall
2-6 Boundary Row
London   SE1 8HN, England

Thomas Nelson Australia
102 Dodds Street
South Melbourne, Victoria 3205, Australia

Nelson Canada
1120 Birchmount Road
Scarborough, Ontario M1K 5G4, Canada

16   15   14   13   12   11   10   9   8   7   6   5   4   3   2

Foreword

The author, Joseph Amendola, a native of New Haven, Connecticut, has been a valued instructor in baking, cake decorating, and ice carving at The Culinary Institute of America since 1950. Prior to that, he taught baking in the Armed Forces and for the Connecticut State Department of Education.

He has tested all the formulas presented in the manual in the bakeshop of the Institute for taste, cost, and acceptance by the public. They are designed for young bakers on the job, for instructors in vocational schools, and for supervisors of baking apprentices.

It is my sincere hope that this manual will be the forerunner of a series of practical teaching aids covering all the phases of quantity cooking and baking and allied subjects now being taught in the vocational schools throughout the land.

For their assistance in arranging this book, the author is greatly indebted to Frances L. Roth and Jacob Tanner. He also wishes to acknowledge the cooperation of Standard Brands, Inc. and General Mills, Inc.

FRANCES L. ROTH,
Director
Culinary Institute of America

Preface

This book has been prepared for the purpose of furnishing essential information and suggestions which will be of assistance to students of baking, as well as to professional bakers. It is designed to increase their knowledge, skill, and information.

This third edition of *The Bakers' Manual* explains the basic recipes and the fundamentals of the art and science of baking even more briefly and accurately than previous editions. A sincere effort has been made to adhere to simple and clear expression and basic terminology, so that the student finds it simple to follow.

If the reader finds the information contained herein of some assistance in his learning baking or in upgrading his baked products, then the efforts spent in preparing this manual will have been well rewarded.

Acknowledgement is made to The Culinary Institue of America, Inc., as well as to all of the baking instructors at C.I.A., for their valuable ideas and suggestions. Sincere thanks are also extended to those who so kindly and constructively helped with the manuscript in the course of preparation. Due to popular demand for the first and second editions of this manual, it has been considered advisable to issue this third revised edition. Every effort has been made to bring this text up-to-date.

JOSEPH AMENDOLA

Contents

Illustrations

TABLES AND GRAPHS

1

Ingredients

FLOUR

Flour is the finely ground meal of wheat and is one of the most important ingredients used in bakery products. Therefore, flour quality has a major influence on the quality of the finished baked products. It is important for the following reasons:

1. It is the backbone and structure of baked goods.
2. It acts as a binding agent and an absorbing agent.
3. It affects the keeping quality of products.
4. It is important to the flavor of products.
5. It adds nutritional value to the baked product.

Wheat

Wheat, from which flour is made, is the most essential grain used in bread-making because it is the only cereal that contains the proper combination of glutenin and gliadin. When flour is combined with water, these properties form gluten, essential for retaining the gas produced by yeast. No other grain can replace wheat in bread making.

The primary types of wheat flour used in baking are hard wheat and soft wheat.

Hard wheat contains a high proportion of gluten, which makes it an excellent choice for breads and breadstuffs. There are several kinds of hard wheat:

1. *One hundred percent straight flour*, a strong flour, is preferred in the production of quality hard rolls and hearth breads. Here it produces the best results.
2. *Patent flour*, generally employed when a formula calls for bread flour, is used in making bread, rolls, and products commonly made with bread flour.
3. *First clear flour* and *second clear flour* are used in making rye breads because of their darker color and higher gluten content.

1

The Milling of Wheat Into Flour

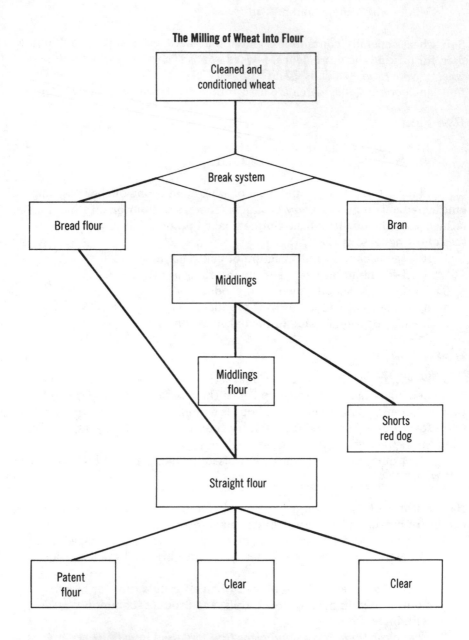

The above diagram shows the general separation of the various grades of flour, but does not show the exact system of the separation of flour streams.

This chart is reprinted from a **Treatise on Cake Making** by permission of Standard Brands, Inc., copyright owner.

4. *Bran* is used mainly in the production of muffins.
5. *Whole wheat flour* (including *graham*) is used primarily in making whole wheat bread and muffins.

Soft wheat generally contains less gluten than hard wheat and is commonly used for making the more delicate baked goods. There are three kinds of soft wheat: *cake flour*, which is used to produce high-quality cakes, and *pastry flour* and *cookie flour*, which are used for pie crusts, cookies, and pastries.

Rye Flour

Rye flour is milled from rye grain. The composition is similar to that of wheat, but the protein or gluten components are quite different.

The protein of rye flour, when made into dough with the addition of water, does not produce gluten as hard wheat does if treated the same way. It is necessary to use some hard wheat flour, such as first or second clear, with rye flour to obtain a porous, well-raised loaf. If rye flour alone is used, the finished product is heavy, somewhat soggy, hard to digest, and unpalatable.

Rye is milled into rye meal or pumpernickel, patent or light rye flour, medium or rye flour, and dark rye flour.

Rye blend is prepared in the mills by mixing a proportion of rye flour with high gluten or clear flour. The proportion of the blend is usually 25 to 40 percent of rye flour to clear flour. The exact amount used depends on local demand and the type of loaf desired. Therefore, the baker must be the judge as to the proper proportions of the blend to be used.

Points of interest concerning the making of rye bread are as follows:
1. Depending on the type of rye bread desired, the formula must be adjusted. A higher proportion of dark rye flour must be used for a heavy dark rye loaf.
2. Rye dough should not be mixed for as long a period as that for light breads.
3. Rye dough should always have a short period of fermentation for the best results.
4. In baking rye bread, steam is required in the oven during the first ten minutes of the baking period.

EGGS

When "eggs" are listed, *whole eggs*—the yolks and the whites—are meant.

Eggs are natural emulsifying agents and so help to produce a smooth batter. This batter may be satisfactorily aerated by creaming or beating, which retains the gases produced by leavening agents.

Heat coagulates eggs at approximately 126°F. This is an important characteristic because such thickening permits eggs to form part of the framework and structure of the product being baked.

Since egg yolks contain fat, they have a shortening action. This is particularly noticeable when eggs are used in sponge cakes and yeast products.

Insofar as leavening action is concerned, egg whites perform the same function as whole eggs. In angel food cake, for example, whipped egg whites produce a foamy mass made of minute air cells which expand when they reach the heat of the oven. Since the egg whites are able to hold air in the batter, the batter increases in volume, and when the heat of the oven hits it, the eggs coagulate and form part of the cell structure of the cake.

Eggs are important because they add color, improve the grain and texture of baked products, increase volume, give structure to the product, add flavor, and have considerable nutritional value. Egg whites figure largely in some of the above points as they are responsible for increasing volume, improving the grain and texture, and giving structure to the product.

There are two types of eggs used in bakeries: shelled eggs and frozen eggs. With few exceptions, both types give the same results in the finished products. In those exceptions, however, shelled eggs produce better results.

Shelled Eggs

Quality eggs must be used to ensure quality in the finished products. Shelled eggs may be converted into weight as follows:

    9 to 11 shelled eggs = 1 lb of whole eggs
    15 to 17 shelled egg whites = 1 lb of egg whites
    22 to 24 shelled egg yolks = 1 lb of egg yolks

Frozen Eggs

Frozen eggs have the following advantages:
1. They save time and labor since breaking and separating are not necessary.
2. They avoid waste through spoilage and other causes.
3. An adequate supply of uniform quality is assured, and uniform quality means better results.

Frozen eggs are sold as whole eggs, yolks, whites, or specials, which contain whole eggs and extra yolks.

SALT

The following are the most important functions performed by salt in baked products:
1. It brings out the desired flavor.
2. It controls yeast action. Increasing the salt content slows the yeast

action but assists in preventing the development of objectionable bacteria and the wild types of yeast which are harmful to the dough.
3. It has a strengthening affect on the gluten in flour. It also helps the dough hold carbon dioxide gas more effectively.
4. It improves the texture and grain of baked products.

MILK

Many different forms of milk are used in the bakery. Following is a list of the types, their origin, or the method of their production:
1. *Liquid whole milk* is milk in its natural form as it comes from the cow.
2. *Liquid skim milk* is produced by removing the butterfat from whole milk.
3. *Buttermilk* is the product that remains after the butterfat has been extracted from the separated cream.
4. *Sweetened condensed whole milk* is made by adding sugar to whole milk, then condensing it (that is, partially evaporating the water from it) until it reaches the required consistency.
5. *Powdered whole and skim milk* is produced in two ways. In the first method, the milk is condensed until a considerable amount of water has been removed. It is then forced through a small opening into a heated chamber where most of the remaining water is removed so that the milk contains only 2½ to 4 percent of moisture. In the second method, the milk is forced through an opening into a heated chamber in which air is being circulated. By this method, the moisture is removed after it leaves the spray.

To reconstitute dry milk powder, water should be added in the following proportions:
Liquid whole milk: 12½ percent solids; 87½ percent water.
Liquid skim milk: 9 percent solids; 91 percent water.

To reconstitute whole milk powder into 1 lb of liquid milk:
16 × 12½% = 2 oz of whole milk powder.
16 × 87½% = 14 oz of water.
Total   16 oz of whole milk.

To reconstitute skim milk powder into 1 lb of liquid skim milk:
16 × 9% = 1.44 oz of skim milk powder.
16 × 91% = 14.56 oz of water.
Total   16 oz of skim milk.

In bakery products, milk improves the texture, food value, keeping quality, and flavor.

SWEETENING AGENTS

Sugar

Cane sugar and beet sugar are both sucrose (sugar) obtained from sugar cane and sugar beets. If refined to the same degree, there is no difference in the sugar whether derived from cane or beets.

Sugar may be secured in the following forms:

1. *Granulated sugar*—the ordinary standard sugar.
2. *Fine granulated sugar*, sometimes called *berry* or *fruit sugar*, is the preferred type of sugar for cake baking. There are several grades known as fine, extra fine, etc.
3. *Confectioner's sugar* (also called *powdered sugar*).
4. *Pulverized sugar*, usually known as *icing sugar*, sometimes contains a small amount of starch to prevent lumping.
5. *Brown sugar*, which contains 85 to 92% sucrose, is used primarily for flavor.

Honey

Honey is a natural invert syrup produced from the nectar of flowers by the honey bee. It varies in composition, depending upon its source. Clover honey is considered one of the best for bakery use since flavor is its primary function.

An average sample of honey contains about 75% invert sugar, 15 to 20% moisture, and a small amount of other substances which give it the delicious flavor.

All lots of honey should be tasted upon delivery to check flavor qualities.

Molasses

Molasses is secured by concentrating the juice of the sugar cane. It contains 35 to 50% sucrose, 20 to 25% water, and the balance of invert sugar, mineral matter, small amounts of protein, and other substances.

Molasses should be checked for flavor before use.

YEAST

Yeast is a microscopic plant or cell grown in vats containing a warm mash of ground corn, barley malt, and water. The two types of yeast are compressed yeast and dry yeast.

If dry yeast is to be replaced by compressed yeast in a formula, approximately 40% of dry yeast by weight is used. For example, if a formula calls for 1 lb of compressed yeast and this must be replaced by dry yeast, 40% of 1 lb, or 6.5 oz of dry yeast, is used. The remaining 60%, or 9.5 oz, is water.

Following are the various reactions of yeast to different temperatures:

60°-70°F	Slow reaction
80°F	Normal reaction
90°-100°F	Fast reaction
138°F	Terminal death point

The ideal storing temperature for yeast is 30°-45°F.

When yeast is mixed with flour into a dough, the yeast plants begin to grow and multiply very fast. This growth produces the leavening gas, or carbon dioxide, which forms the small bubbles that cause the dough to rise.

Yeast in baked products increases the volume and improves the grain, the texture, and the flavor.

CHEMICAL LEAVENERS

Chemical leaveners may be divided into two classes: acids, such as bicarbonate of soda or baking powder, and ammonium carbonate.

Acid leaveners. In the case of baking powder, an acid-reacting salt or a combination of such salts acts upon sodium bicarbonate in the presence of moisture and heat, releasing carbon dioxide gas, which leavens the product. Sodium bicarbonate contains carbon and oxygen, which form carbon dioxide gas. Hence, the reaction is similar whether a baking powder is used containing both the acid component and the sodium bicarbonate, or whether the sodium bicarbonate is added to a batter which has sufficient acidity in other ingredients to release the gas from the sodium bicarbonate.

An example of this is the addition of sodium bicarbonate to spice cakes containing molasses. The molasses is acid and is able to release the carbon dioxide gas from the added sodium bicarbonate.

Ammonium carbonate is a little different in its action. Like sodium bicarbonate, it also contains the constituents of carbon dioxide gas. Unlike the acid type, however, it does not require an acid or other substance to cause a reaction. Carbon dioxide gas is liberated from the ammonium carbonate by decomposition due to heat and moisture in the baking process. Since it decomposes rapidly, it is used primarily in cream puffs and cookies, where a sudden expansion is desirable.

Chemical leaveners used in baked products improve their grain and texture; they bring about more uniform symmetry, and increase volume.

FATS AND SHORTENINGS

Fats used for baking purposes are all edible fats or hydrogenated oils of vegetable or animal origin such as hydrogenated shortening, lard oils, butter, and oleomargarine.

The Action of Baking Powder

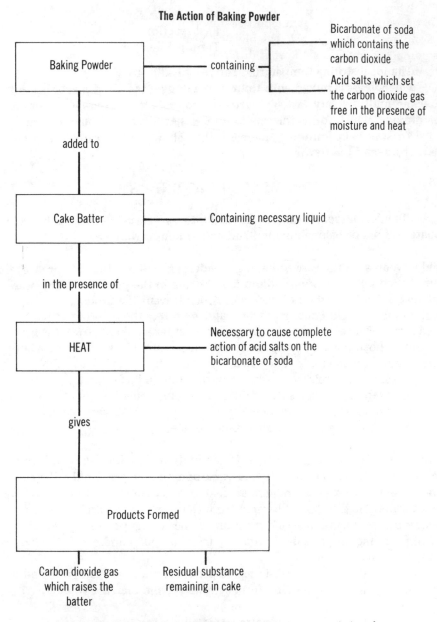

This chart is reprinted from a **Treatise on Cake Making** by permission of Standard Brands, Inc., copyright owner.

Oleomargarine and butter are two special types of fat. Margarine is made from animal or vegetable oils or a combination of both.

Whereas other types of fats are usually bland, butter and margarine are used primarily for their characteristic flavors which they impart to the products in which they are used. The physical properties of the fats of which they are composed are also somewhat different. This makes them "melt in the mouth," and this characteristic is imparted to the products in which they are used, particularly in icings, thus improving the quality.

Lard, the rendered fat of hogs, is used primarily in bread and pie dough.

Oils are liquid fats used, within limits, for deep fat frying in bakeries, and also as a wash for different types of rolls, and for greasing pans.

Compounds are part lard and part vegetable fat.

Shortenings are all those solidified fats other than lard, butter, and oleomargarine. They do not dissolve in the liquid of the cake batter. Instead, they mix with the other ingredients, covering them uniformly with a fine film or dispersing through the mixture in fine globules. They form an emulsion with the eggs, liquids, and other ingredients.

One of the greatest advantages of using the emulsifying type of shortening in cake making is its ability to form a more stable emulsion and permit the inclusion of greater amounts of moisture and other ingredients without breaking down the batter.

To ensure that the shortenings being used will contribute quality characteristics to the baked product, the following points should be considered:

1. *Consistency of plasticity.* To permit shortening to function properly, it must be thoroughly and uniformly distributed in the dough or batter. It should be of a consistency which will mix easily into the dough or batter. It should also be easy to handle in the bake shop—not too hard or brittle in cold weather, nor too soft in warm weather.
2. *Flavor, color, and odor* are very important. With the exception of butter, lard, and margarine, most high grade shortenings are bland in flavor and light in color. All shortenings should be free from foreign odor.
3. *Keeping quality* of shortenings must be satisfactory under the storage conditions available in the bakery. The very best shortenings can be spoiled by rancidity when stored improperly or for too long. Shortenings must be kept in a cool place and tightly covered to keep out as much air as possible.

Puff paste shortening is used mostly in the making of Danish pastry, various puff paste articles, and as a replacement for butter in some kinds of coffee cakes. Most of the puff paste shortening is made from vegetable oils combined with hydrogenated coconut oil. The finished product then will have different degrees of hardness, depending upon the purpose for which it is intended.

Functions of Fats in Bakery Products

Fats function in several ways in bakery products:
1. They increase the tenderness of the product.
2. They increase the quality of the product, both for keeping and eating.
3. They enhance the food value of the product.
4. They improve the grain and texture.

FLAVORING MATERIALS

Although these materials cannot be considered as truly basic ingredients in cake making or other bakery products, they are important in producing the most desirable flavor.

Flavoring materials can be divided into three categories: extracts, emulsions, and dried spices. These and others, such as chocolate, give the desired flavor to better varieties of baked products.

Flavoring extracts are usually an alcoholic solution of the natural oils and other substances contained in the actual flavoring. Lemon and vanilla extracts are probably the best known and most widely used.

Flavoring emulsions are prepared by combining the natural oils and other substances containing the flavor with a certain amount of gum and water. Lemon flavor, as well as being used as an extract, is the most popular emulsion used in bakeries.

Artificial flavorings and combinations of natural and artificial flavors, are produced both in the form of extracts and emulsions. Because of the potency of artificial flavors, care should be taken to avoid their excessive use.

Spices consist of any of the seeds, fruit, roots, buds, blossoms, or bark of certain flavor-producing plants which possess natural flavoring properties. They can lose their strength with age so they should always be kept in tightly sealed containers. The principal spices used are nutmeg, ginger, cinnamon, clove, mace, and allspice.

Salt may be classed as a flavoring material for our purposes. Since it intensifies other flavors, it should be mentioned as a very important flavoring material.

Chocolate and cocoa are derived from the cocoa bean and may be loosely classified as spices although, of course, they do not fit this classification. The principal difference in these products is the removal from cocoa of the cocoa butter, part of the natural fat, before the cocoa is powdered. Cocoa made by the Dutch process of manufacture is slightly darker and stronger in flavor than that produced by other methods.

Use of Flavoring

Inferior flavoring material impairs the quality of any baked product and should be avoided. Excessive use, except in the case of cocoa or chocolate, is a common error. Bakers work in an atmosphere where flavoring odors are strong and they frequently become immune to the taste and flavor. If they do not measure the quantity of flavoring material carefully, they tend to increase the amount until the product has that "bakery taste" common to some baked products.

In order to avoid the excessive use of flavoring materials, those which are particularly strong should be diluted with a suitable liquid. If the flavoring or spice is in dry form, it should be mixed with sugar. This method will permit more accurate measurement.

The flavor of the finished product is so important that it is foolish to be careless with regard to the quality and quantity of flavoring materials. Carelessness in this respect means that the baker is gambling with the loss of customers as well as with the expensive ingredients used in the product.

2

Yeast-Made Products

BREAD, ROLLS, COFFEE CAKE, AND DANISH PASTRY

Bread is one of the most essential products made by bakers. It is a nutritious food, obtainable at low cost, and an essential part of every family's daily food requirement.

Many beginners in the baking trade are not enthusiastic about making bread and rolls because they feel the results are not as attractive as pastries and that breads do not produce large profits. However, the commercial bakeries are doing a fine job in giving the public excellent quality breads.

In addition to standard breads, there are specialty breads and rolls, some of which have eye appeal and flavor to please the most fastidious gourmet. Examples of some of these may be found on the following pages.

Following are six important rules to follow in making bread and rolls.
1. Strict personal cleanliness for all employees in the bakery.
2. Clean utensils, materials, and machinery.
3. Use the very best quality of ingredients.
4. Keep a dough thermometer on hand for controlling dough temperatures.
5. Read all formulas carefully and scale all ingredients properly.
6. Serve only fresh products which are baked daily.

BREAD AND DOUGH PRODUCTION STAGES

There are a dozen steps to baking bread, listed below. Some of them are obvious and require no further explanation; others are elaborated in the text that follows.

1. Start with raw materials
2. Weigh ingredients
3. Mix
4. Fermentation period
5. Scaling
6. Rounding
7. Bench proofing
8. Molding
9. Panning
10. Pan proofing
11. Baking
12. Cooling

Dough Mixing

There are three principal reasons for dough mixing:
1. To bring about a uniform mixture of ingredients and to form a smooth dough.
2. To develop the gluten in the dough mass in order to promote the elasticity of the dough and permit it to retain the gases formed by the yeast.
3. To distribute the yeast cells uniformly so that they will receive proper nutrition.

There are two principal methods of mixing dough:

Sponge dough method. Part of the flour, water, yeast, sugar, and shortening are mixed, forming a dough called the "sponge." This is permitted to rise and ferment to the desired point. The sponge is then put back into the mixer and combined with the balance of the ingredients—the remainder of the flour, water, sugar, salt, milk, shortening, and yeast. After this is all mixed together into a smooth dough it is again allowed to rise and divided into various sized pieces. The sponge dough is suitable for the larger commercial operations.

Straight dough method. All the ingredients are placed into the mixing bowl and mixed in a single operation. The dough is then allowed to rise, the length of time depending upon the type of dough.

Fermentation

This takes place after the dough has been mixed and up until the time that the oven in which the dough is to be baked reaches a temperature of 138°F. At this point the yeast bacteria are killed and fermentation ceases.

The most favorable temperature in which fermentation can take place is 80° to 82°F. The length of the fermentation period depends upon the amount of yeast in the dough and the temperature of the room; the lower this temperature, the slower the fermentation.

A dough that is not sufficiently fermented (underproofed) is referred to as "young dough"; dough that is overproofed is known as "old dough."

The gases developed during fermentation (carbon dioxide) are forced out of the dough by a process known as "punching" the dough; this aids in relaxing the gluten and equalizes the temperature of the dough.

Bread Ingredients and Their Functions

Ingredients	Binding agent	Absorbing agent	Aids keeping qualities	Backbone and structure	Affects eating qualities	Nutritional value	Affects flavor	Affects fermentation	Affects gluten	Texture and grain	Imparts crust color	Affects symmetry	Volume	Produces tenderness	Adds quality to product
Bread flour	X	X	X	X	X	X	X								
Salt							X	X	X	X					
Sugar			X		X	X	X	X			X	X			
Shortening			X		X	X				X				X	X
Milk solids			X			X	X			X					X
Water	X														
Yeast							X			X			X		

The best time to "punch" the dough is when it has doubled in size through fermentation. To test if the dough is ready for punching, insert the open hand into the dough four or five inches. If the dough recedes, it is ready for punching. If it springs back when the hand is inserted, longer fermentation is required. After the dough is punched, it must be proofed a second time before being made up into bread or rolls.

Controlling Dough Temperatures

Controlling dough temperatures is very important. Proper fermentation, the quality of the finished product, and efficient production depend greatly on the temperature of the dough from the time it is mixed until it is baked.

The most desirable temperature for sponge and straight doughs range between 76° and 80°F. The exact temperature selected depends upon shop conditions and the type of bread desired. It is, therefore, highly important to calculate the required temperature of the water and the amount of ice or cooling needed to obtain the desired temperature for either sponge or straight dough.

The various types of dough mixers have different types of agitator areas and cooling devices. The machine allowance and friction differential depend on the type of mixer used as well as the amount of dough. To determine the amount of heat generated by the friction of the mixer, the following method may be used:

Mix the dough, noting the exact temperature of the flour, water, and the room. After the dough is properly mixed, note its temperature. Next, multiply the dough temperature by three, because you are working with three factors: flour, water, and room temperature. Next, subtract the sum of the three temperatures, flour, water, and room, from the dough temperature multiplied by three. The result will be the heat of the friction generated by the mixer.

Dough temperature	79°F
Multiplied by 3	237°F
Flour temperature	69°F
Water temperature	64°F
Room temperature	79°F
	212°F
Subtract	237°F
	−212°F
Mixer machine friction	25°F

Mixing time is also an element which governs the amount of friction and should be taken into consideration when calculating temperatures. Now that

Ordinary Bread Faults and Their Causes

Faults \ Causes	Improper mixing	Insufficient salt	Too much salt	Dough weight too much for pan	Dough weight too light for pan	Insufficient yeast	Dough proofed too much	Dough underproofed	Dough temperature too high	Dough temperature too low	Dough too stiff	Proof box too hot	Green flour	Dough chilled	Too much sugar	Insufficient sugar	Dough too young	Dough too old	Improper molding	Insufficient shortening	Oven temperature too high	Oven temperature too low	Over-baked
Lack of volume	X		X		X	X		X						X			X	X			X		
Too much volume		X		X			X											X				X	
Crust color too pale										X		X				X		X					
Crust color too dark										X											X		
Crust blisters															X		X	X					
Shelling of top crust		X						X			X		X			X	X		X				
Poor keeping qualities							X		X		X		X			X		X		X		X	
Poor texture, crumbly							X					X						X				X	
Crust too thick																X	X	X				X	X
Streaky crumb																			X				
Gray crumb							X	X	X			X											
Lack of shred					X		X	X									X	X					
Coarse grain	X									X							X	X	X				
Poor taste and flavor		X							X									X					

the heat of the mixer friction has been established, the desired temperature of a dough with water as a chief factor must be determined.

Dough temperature desired	80°F
Multiplied by 3	240°F
Machine friction	25°F
Flour temperature	75°F
Room temperature	75°F
	175°F
Subtract	240°F
	−175°F
Water temperature required	65°F

When a sponge dough is to be mixed, the sponge temperature must be added to the total temperature of flour, room, and mixer friction. This means working with four factors and the desired dough temperature must be multiplied by four.

Dough temperature desired	80°F
Multiplied by 4	320°F
Machine friction	25°F
Sponge temperature	80°F
Flour temperature	70°F
Room temperature	80°F
	255°F
Subtract	320°F
	−255°F
Water temperature required	65°F

Often it is necessary to use ice to lower the water temperature to the degree required. In that case, the amount of ice necessary must be determined. For example, suppose 24 lb of water are required at a temperature of 54°F and the tap water available is 64°F. How much ice must be used?

64°F less 54°F	10°F
10°F multiplied by 24 lb	240 lb

It takes 144 BTU's (British Thermal Units) of heat to melt 1 lb of ice to 1 lb of water. Therefore, we divide the 240 lb by 144 BTU's and find that we must use 1 2/3 lb of ice and 22 1/3 lb of tap water at 64°F to reach a temperature of 54°F.

Water Temperature Chart

The chart below may be used for mixing dough with a desired dough temperature of 80°F and a machine friction of 25°F.

Read horizontally for flour temperature, vertically for room temperature. Where the two rows of figures meet determines the water temperature required. In the example below, the room temperature is 76°F and the flour temperature is 78°F. Therefore, the required water temperature is 61°F.

Room Temperatures

	90	88	86	84	82	80	78	76	74	72	70	68	66	64	62	60	58
90	35	37	39	41	43	45	47	49	51	53	55	57	59	61	63	65	67
88	37	39	41	43	45	47	49	51	53	55	57	59	61	63	65	67	69
86	39	41	43	45	47	49	51	53	55	57	59	61	63	65	67	69	71
84	41	43	45	47	49	51	53	55	57	59	61	63	65	67	69	71	73
82	43	45	47	49	51	53	55	57	59	61	63	65	67	69	71	73	75
80	45	47	49	51	53	55	57	59	61	63	65	67	69	71	73	75	77
78	47	49	51	53	55	57	59	(61)	63	65	67	69	71	73	75	77	79
76	49	51	53	55	57	59	61	63	65	67	69	71	73	75	77	79	81
74	51	53	55	57	59	61	63	65	67	69	71	73	75	77	79	81	83
72	53	55	57	59	61	63	65	67	69	71	73	75	77	79	81	83	85
70	55	57	59	61	63	65	67	69	71	73	75	77	79	81	83	85	87
68	57	59	61	63	65	67	69	71	73	75	77	79	81	83	85	87	89
66	59	61	63	65	67	69	71	73	75	77	79	81	83	85	87	89	91
64	61	63	65	67	69	71	73	75	77	79	81	83	85	87	89	91	93

Flour Temperatures (vertical axis label)

Determining Water Temperatures for Making Bread

WHITE PAN BREAD

Bread flour	10 lb	
Sugar		6 oz
Malt		4 oz
Salt		4 oz
Nonfat dry milk solids		8 oz
Water (3 1/8 qt)	6 lb	4 oz
Yeast		8 oz
Shortening		6 oz
	18 lb	8 oz

Method: Straight dough. 1 hour fermentation period.
Baking instructions: 400°F.

RYE BREAD

Rye blend flour	5 lb	
Salt		2 oz
Sugar		2 oz
Shortening		2 oz
Water (1½ qt)	3 lb	
Yeast		4 oz
Caraway seeds		1 oz
Rye flavor*		1 oz
	8 lb	12 oz

Method: Straight dough. Mix for 5 minutes at second speed. Desired dough
temperature, 80°F. 1 hour fermentation period.
Scaling instructions: Rolls: 1 lb per dozen. Bread: 1 lb per loaf.
Baking instructions: 400°F with steam for the first 10 minutes.

JEWISH CHALAH

Bread flour	5 lb	
Salt		1½ oz
Sugar or malt		4 oz
Oil		4 oz
Egg yolks, 6		4 oz
Yeast		3 oz
Water (1 3/8 qt)	2 lb	12 oz
	8 lb	12½ oz

*May be omitted

Method: Straight dough. Mix for approximately 12 minutes at second speed.
        Desired dough temperature, 80°F. 1 hour fermentation period. Egg
        wash before baking. Braiding instructions follow on pages 21
        through 25.
Scaling instructions: 1 lb per loaf.
Baking instructions: 400°F.

WHOLE WHEAT BREAD AND ROLLS

Whole wheat flour	5 lb	
Salt		2 oz
Sugar		8 oz
Shortening		8 oz
Milk solids		4 oz
Water (1 11/16 qt)	3 lb	6 oz
Yeast		4 oz
	10 lb	

Method: Straight dough. Mix approximately 12 minutes at medium speed.
        Desired dough temperature, 80°F. 1 hour fermentation period.
        Remove from pans after baking.
Scaling instructions: Rolls: 1 lb per dozen. Bread: 1 lb per loaf.
Baking instructions: 400°F.

PUMPERNICKEL BREAD

Rye flour	2 lb	8 oz
Bread flour, clear	2 lb	8 oz
Rye meal	1 lb	8 oz
Salt		2 oz
Sugar or malt		2 oz
Water (2 qt)	4 lb	
Yeast		3 oz
Rye flavor		1 oz
	11 lb	

Method: Straight dough. Mix approximately 5 minutes at medium speed.
        Desired dough temperature, 80°F. 30 minute fermentation period.
        Wash with paste of rye and water before baking. Punch holes before
        baking.
Baking instructions: 400°F with steam the first 10 minutes.

Steps For Making Two-Braided Bread

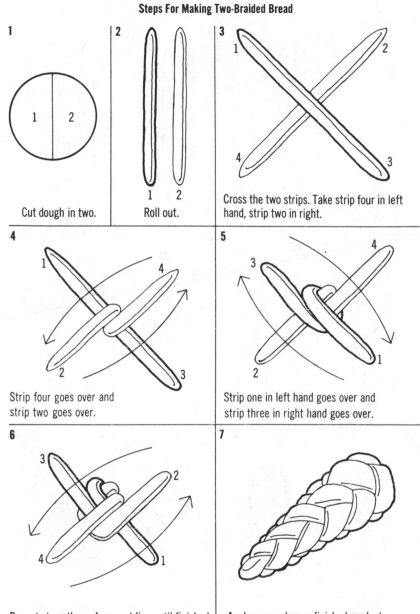

1 Cut dough in two.

2 Roll out.

3 Cross the two strips. Take strip four in left hand, strip two in right.

4 Strip four goes over and strip two goes over.

5 Strip one in left hand goes over and strip three in right hand goes over.

6 Repeat steps three, four, and five until finished.

7 Apply eggwash over finished product.

Steps For Making Three-Braided Bread

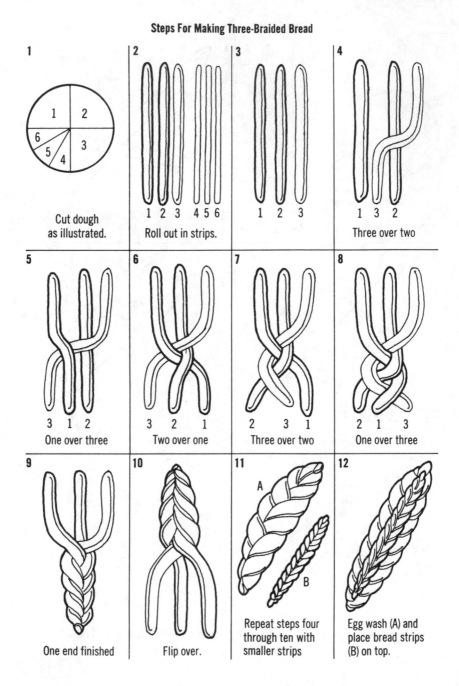

1 Cut dough as illustrated.

2 Roll out in strips. 1 2 3 4 5 6

3 1 2 3

4 1 3 2 — Three over two

5 3 1 2 — One over three

6 3 2 1 — Two over one

7 2 3 1 — Three over two

8 2 1 3 — One over three

9 One end finished

10 Flip over.

11 Repeat steps four through ten with smaller strips

12 Egg wash (A) and place bread strips (B) on top.

Steps For Making Four-Braided Bread

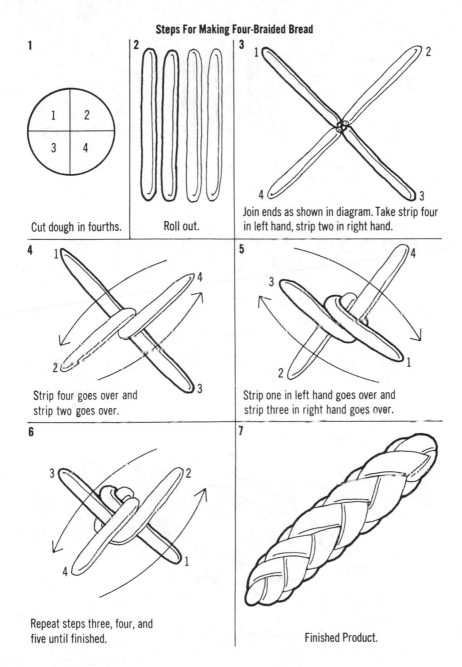

1 Cut dough in fourths.

2 Roll out.

3 Join ends as shown in diagram. Take strip four in left hand, strip two in right hand.

4 Strip four goes over and strip two goes over.

5 Strip one in left hand goes over and strip three in right hand goes over.

6 Repeat steps three, four, and five until finished.

7 Finished Product.

Steps For Making Five-Braided Bread

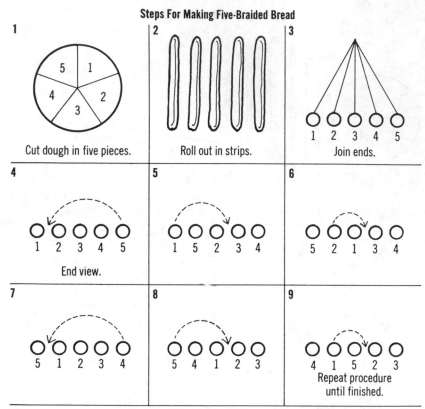

1 Cut dough in five pieces.

2 Roll out in strips.

3 Join ends.

4 End view.

5

6

7

8

9 Repeat procedure until finished.

10

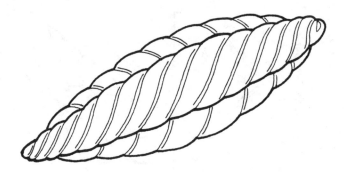

Finished Product.

Steps For Making Six-Braided Bread

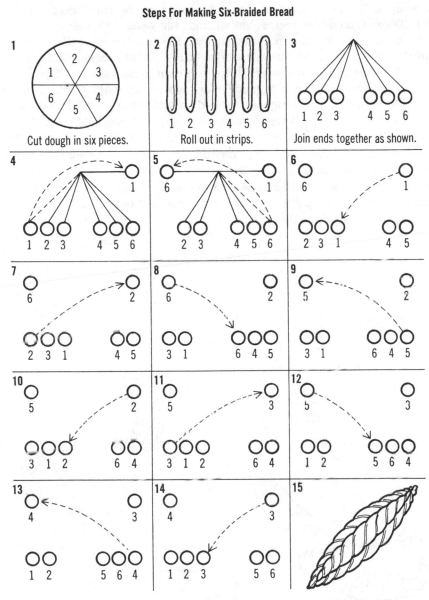

1 Cut dough in six pieces.

2 Roll out in strips.

3 Join ends together as shown.

Repeat procedure until finished.

Finished Product.

Cornucopia. The Cornucopia or Horn of Plenty is made from bread dough, using the hard roll dough recipe, but without the yeast. This method for making the cornucopia is rather new and unique; the dough is not rolled out manually, but is extruded through a meat grinder, with a sausage funnel attached to it in order for the dough to be symmetrically shaped. The form for the cornucopia can be made in any size, using chicken wire covered with aluminum foil. The dough is wrapped around the form of the cornucopia. Note that the dough is started from the small end, working toward the large opening of the cornucopia. It is recommended that a rich egg wash be used over the dough before baking. A good glaze for the finished cornucopia can be prepared by using ½ ounce of granulated powdered gelatin and 1 pint of water. The gelatin should be heated and dissolved and brushed or applied directly on the cornucopia directly after it comes out of the oven. This will give the product a shiny effect.

Steps in Making a Cornucopia

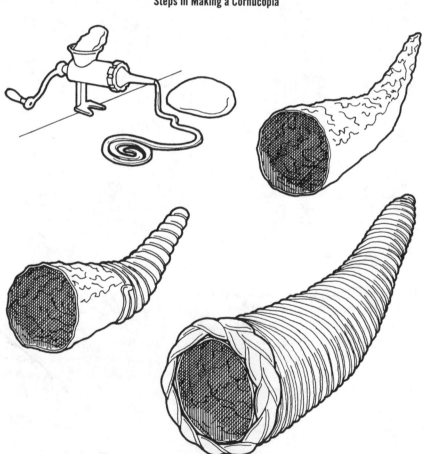

HARD ROLL DOUGH

Bread flour	5 lb	
Salt		2 oz
Sugar		2 oz
Shortening		2 oz
Egg whites		2 oz
Water (1½ qt)	3 lb	
Yeast		3 oz
	8 lb	11 oz

Method: Straight dough. Mix approximately 12 minutes at second speed. Desired dough temperature, 80°F. 1 hour fermentation period.
Scaling instructions: Hard rolls: 1 lb per dozen. Bread: 1 lb per loaf.
Baking instructions: 400°F with steam for approximately the first 10 minutes.

Variations: This dough may be used for a variety of hard rolls, French bread, Vienna bread, or Italian bread.

HOME-MADE EGG NOODLES

Bread flour	5 lb	
Eggs, 16	1 lb	8 oz
Salt		2 oz
Oil		1 oz
Water (1 pint)	1 lb	
	7 lb	11 oz

Method: Mix into a smooth dough and let relax for approximately one-half hour before rolling. Let dry and cut. This dough lends itself to the making of baskets and horns of plenty.

WEAVING BREAD OR NOODLE BASKETS

The art of weaving bread or noodle dough requires patient practice. Many important points influence the finished product.

Most important is to have a well-made frame or board. There should be an uneven number of holes, as shown in the illustrations on page 28. There are always an uneven number of pegs spread approximately three-quarters of an inch to one inch apart, and these are set at a slight angle so that the basket is larger at the top than at the bottom. Note that there are three different graduated-size holes in the illustrations.

The dough being used must be rolled evenly and woven around the wooden pegs for uniformity.

Before baking, brush with a straight egg wash. The handle may be made with wire. Weave the dough around the wire, bake, and then set on to the basket.

Boards for weaving bread baskets. Each row is for a different size basket.

Bread basket being woven.

SOFT ROLL DOUGH

Bread flour	5 lb	
Salt		2 oz
Sugar		8 oz
Shortening		8 oz
Milk solids		4 oz
Water (1½ qt)	3 lb	
Yeast		4 oz
	9 lb	10 oz

Method: Straight dough. Mix approximately 12 minutes at medium speed. Desired dough temperature, 80°F. 1 hour fermentation period.
Scaling instructions: 12 oz per dozen rolls. Yield: 12½ dozen.
Baking instructions: 400°F.

DANISH PASTRY DOUGH

Salt		1 oz
Sugar	1 lb	
Butter	2 lb	10 oz
Eggs	1 lb	
Milk (1 qt)	2 lb	
Yeast		4 oz
Bread flour	4lb	8 oz
Cake flour		8 oz
	11 lb	15 oz

Method: Mix all ingredients but 2 lb of butter into a straight dough. Roll the 2 lb of butter into the dough. After mixing, retard 10 to 15 minutes. Then sheet out dough to a thickness of ½ to ¾ inch, three times as long as wide. Spot butter over 2/3 the length of the dough sheet. Fold the third without butter over the center third. Fold the remaining third on top, making three layers of dough, two layers with butter. Again allow the dough to rest 20 to 30 minutes in the retarder. This rolling and folding must be repeated twice more. After rolling out for the last time, it is advisable to allow the dough to rest in the retarder for 4 or 5 hours before making up into varieties. Proofing before baking should be with little steam and at 90° to 95°F.
Baking instructions: 375°F.

Bread Alligator

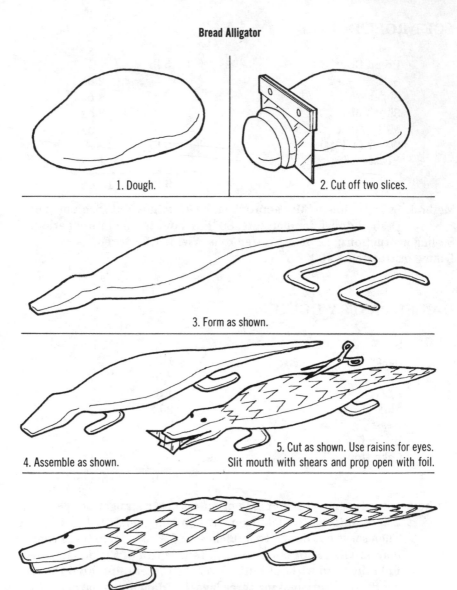

1. Dough.

2. Cut off two slices.

3. Form as shown.

4. Assemble as shown.

5. Cut as shown. Use raisins for eyes.
Slit mouth with shears and prop open with foil.

6. Finished bread Alligator.

Bread Turtle

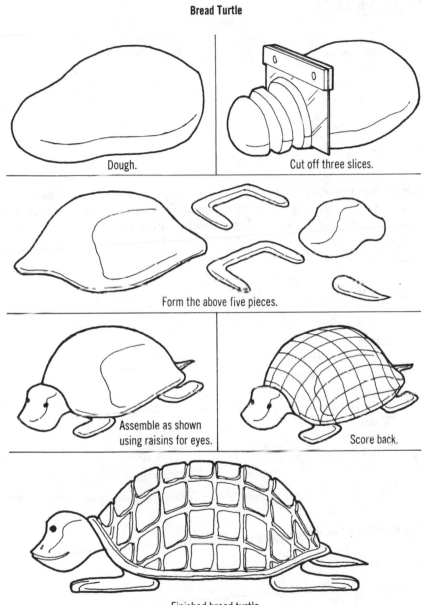

Dough.

Cut off three slices.

Form the above five pieces.

Assemble as shown using raisins for eyes.

Score back.

Finished bread turtle.

BANANA BREAD

Sugar	2 lb	
Shortening	1 lb	
Salt		1 oz
Eggs, beaten	1 lb	8 oz
Bananas, mashed	2 lb	8 oz
Cake flour	3 lb	
Cream of tartar		1 oz
Baking soda		1 oz
	10 lb	3 oz

Method: Cream together sugar shortening, and salt. Add beaten eggs and bananas. Sift together flour, cream of tartar, and baking soda; add to other ingredients and mix together until smooth.

Scaling instructions: 1½ lb per loaf.

Baking instructions: 375°F.

SWEET DOUGH

Salt		1 oz
Sugar	1 lb	
Shortening and butter	1 lb	
Flavor and spice (to taste)		
Eggs		12 oz
Milk (1 qt)	2 lb	
Yeast		6 oz
Bread flour	3 lb	8 oz
Cake flour	1 lb	
	9 lb	11 oz

Method: Mix into a straight dough. 1½ hr fermentation period. Desired dough temperature, 80°F.

Baking instructions: 375°F.

DATE AND NUT BREAD

Brown sugar	1 lb	
Shortening		8 oz
Salt		1 oz
Eggs		12 oz
Baking soda		1 oz
Water (1 qt)	2 lb	
Bread flour	2 lb	
Whole wheat flour	1 lb	
Baking powder		1 oz

Dates, soaked and chopped	2 lb	
Walnuts	1 lb	
	10 lb	7 oz

Method: Cream together sugar, shortening, and salt. Beat in eggs. Dissolve baking soda in water and add. Sift together flours and baking powder, add to mixture, and mix until smooth. Flour dates, and then stir into dough with walnuts.

Scaling instructions: 1 lb 6 oz per loaf.

Baking instructions: 375°F.

CORN BREAD

Cornmeal	2 lb	4 oz
Pastry flour	1 lb	8 oz
Sugar		4 oz
Baking powder		1½ oz
Salt		1¼ oz
Milk (1½ qt)	3 lb	
Eggs		12 oz
Butter, melted		12 oz
	8 lb	11 oz

Method: Sift cornmeal, flour, sugar, baking powder, and salt, and blend together. Beat milk and eggs together and add. Add melted butter and mix smooth. Pour mixture into greased sheet pans.

Scaling instructions: 9 lb 7 oz for one 18 X 24-inch sheet pan.

Baking instructions: 450°F. Serve hot.

BASIC FRUIT MUFFINS

Sugar, powdered	1 lb	
Shortening and butter		8 oz
Salt		½ oz
Eggs	1 lb	
Milk (1 pint)	1 lb	
Baking powder		1 oz
Cake flour	1 lb	12 oz
Fruit or nuts	1 lb	8 oz
	6 lb	13½ oz

Method: Cream together sugar, shortening, and salt. Add eggs, then milk. Sift baking powder and flour together and mix into mixture until smooth. Fold fruit or nuts into mixture.

Scaling instructions: 18 oz per dozen.

Baking instructions: 400°F.

Varieties of Bread

1 = Long pumpernickel. 2 = Italian bread. 3 = American rye. 4 = Pullman loaf. 5 = Round cinnamon loaf. 6 = Braided loaf. 7 = French loaf. 8 = Jewish Challah. 9 = Six-strand braided loaf. 10 = Vienna loaf. 11 = Round pumpernickel. 12 = White Mountain bread. 13 = White pan bread.

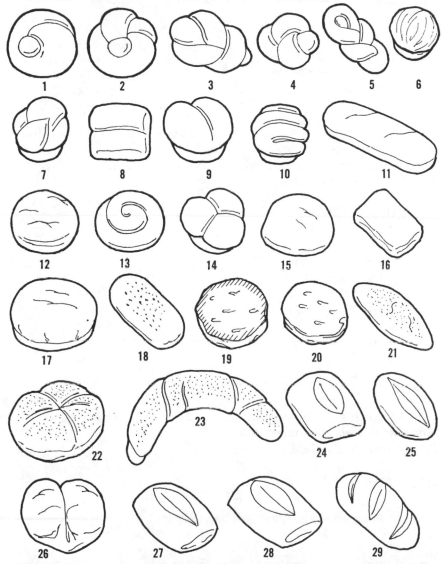

Soft rolls: 1 = Single knot. 2 = Double knot. 3 = Figure eight. 4 = Square knot. 5 = Braided roll. 6 = Spiral butter roll. 7 = Butter twist. 8 = Parker house roll. 9 = Twin roll. 10 = Butter roll. 11 = Frankfurter roll. 12 = Whole wheat roll. 13 = Spiral roll. 14 = Clover leaf roll. 15 = Pan roll. 16 = Snowflake roll. 17 = Hamburger roll. 18 = Poppyseed roll. 19 = Maryland roll with flour top. 20 = Vienna roll without flour top. 21 = Vienna bridge roll. **Hard rolls:** 22 = Kaiser roll. 23 = Crescent roll. 24 = French roll. 25 = Rye roll. 26 = Water roll. 27 = Small French roll. 28 = Club roll. 29 = Rye roll.

BAKING POWDER BISCUITS

Cake flour	2 lb	
Salt		1 oz
Baking powder		2 oz
Shortening and butter		12 oz
Milk (1¼ pint)	1 lb	4 oz
	4 lb	3 oz

Method: Sift and blend flour, salt, and baking powder. Rub in shortening and butter. Add milk and mix smooth.

Scaling instructions: Approximately 4 dozen 2-inch biscuits.

Baking instructions: 400°F.

BRIOCHES

Flour	1 lb	8 oz
Yeast		2 oz
Milk (1 pint)	1 lb	
Salt		1 oz
Sugar		2 oz
Butter	1 lb	4 oz
Eggs		12 oz
Flour	1 lb	12 oz
	6 lb	9 oz

Method: Make a sponge of flour, yeast, and milk and let rise. Mix in remaining ingredients until smooth. Place in the refrigerator overnight.

Scaling instructions: 1½ oz per unit.

Baking instructions: 375°F.

POPOVERS

Eggs		8 oz
Milk (1 pint)	1 lb	
Salt		½ oz
Sugar		½ oz
Bread flour		12 oz
	2 lb	5 oz

Method: Beat well together eggs, milk, salt, and sugar. Add flour and mix until smooth.

Scaling instructions: Grease every other cup of muffin pan to allow for expansion of popovers. Fill muffin cups three quarters full. Only 6 popovers should be placed in the pan instead of the full 12. Yield: 36 medium-size popovers.

Baking instructions: 400°-425°F for 10 minutes. Reduce heat to 375°F for additional 20 minutes. Be sure to dry popovers sufficiently before removing from oven to prevent them from collapsing.

WAFFLES

Eggs		6 oz
Sugar (variable)		2 oz
Salt		¼ oz
Milk (1 pint)	1 lb	
Cake flour	1 lb	
Baking powder		1 oz
Butter, melted		4 oz
	2 lb	13¼ oz

Method: Beat together eggs, sugar, and salt. Add milk. Sift flour and baking powder, and stir in until batter is smooth. Add melted butter.

Variation: For cornmeal waffles, replace 4 oz of flour with 4 oz of cornmeal.

GINGERBREAD WAFFLES

Molasses	1 lb	
Shortening		5 oz
Eggs, 4		
Salt		¼ oz
Baking soda		½ oz
Ginger		¾ oz
Buttermilk (½ pint)		8 oz
Pastry flour	1 lb	
	2 lb	14½ oz

Method: Melt shortening and mix with molasses. Whip together eggs, salt, baking soda, and ginger, and add to molasses mixture. Add buttermilk. Sift flour and add to mixture and mix smooth. Waffle iron should be slightly cooler for this type of waffle.

CORN BREAD AND CORN BREAD STICKS

Salt		2 oz
Sugar		3 oz
Shortening		8 oz
Cake flour	2 lb	8 oz
Yellow cornmeal	2 lb	8 oz

Baking powder		5 oz
Eggs, whole	1 lb	8 oz
Buttermilk (2 qt)	4 lb	
	11 lb	10 oz

Method: Blend salt, sugar, shortening, flour, cornmeal, and baking powder
and mix. Beat in eggs and 2 lb of buttermilk until mixture is smooth.
Add rest of buttermilk and mix with above in three parts. Press into
corn sticks with star tube.

GRIDDLE CAKES

Eggs, 3		5 oz
Salt		¼ oz
Sugar (variable)		1 oz
Milk (1½ pints)	1 lb	8 oz
Cake flour	1 lb	
Baking powder		1 oz
Butter, melted		2 oz
	3 lb	1¼ oz

Method: Beat together the eggs, salt, and sugar. Add milk. Sift flour and
baking powder and blend with other ingredients. Add melted butter
and mix in well. Care should be taken not to overmix griddle cake
batter as this tends to make them tough.

FRENCH CRESCENTS

Milk (1 qt)	2 lb	
Yeast		3 oz
Salt		1¼ oz
Sugar		3 oz
Butter		5 oz
Bread flour	3 lb	8 oz
Butter	1 lb	8 oz
	7 lb	12¼ oz

Method: Mix all ingredients except the butter and stir into a smooth dough.
Roll butter into the dough, giving 3 turns as for Danish. Allow to
rest in refrigerator overnight. Roll pieces into crescent shapes, proof
in proofing cabinet and bake.
Scaling instructions: 1½ oz per unit.
Baking instructions: 375°F.

BOSTON BROWN BREAD

Bread flour	1 lb	
Rye flour	1 lb	
Whole wheat flour	1 lb	
Cornmeal	1 lb	
Salt		2 oz
Cream of tartar		1 oz
Molasses	1 lb	
Eggs		4 oz
Milk (2 qt)	4 lb	
Baking soda		2 oz
	9 lb	9 oz

Method: Sift and blend the flours and cornmeal, salt, and cream of tartar. Beat together molasses, eggs, and 3 lb of milk, and add to dry ingredients. Dissolve the baking soda in the rest of the milk and mix smooth.

Scaling instructions: Line pans with paper, 4 lb 8 oz per 4½ × 4½ × 14½-inch pan. Fill pans approximately two-thirds full.

Baking instructions: Steam 2 hours at 450°F.

Raisin brown bread: Add 1 lb of raisins.

CORN MUFFINS AND CORN STICKS

Sugar	1 lb	
Shortening		8 oz
Salt		½ oz
Eggs		8 oz
Milk (1½ pints)	1 lb	8 oz
Cornmeal	1 lb	
Pastry flour	1 lb	8 oz
Baking powder		1½ oz
	6 lb	2 oz

Method: Cream sugar, shortening, and salt. Beat in eggs and stir in milk. Add cornmeal. Sift flour and baking powder and mix into above until smooth.

Scaling instructions: 1½ lb per dozen. Yield: Approximately 4 dozen muffins or 6 dozen corn sticks.

Baking instructions: 425°F.

PIZZA DOUGH

Bread flour	3 lb	
Salt		1 oz
Oil or shortening		4 oz
Yeast*		1½ oz
Water (1 qt)	2 lb	
	5 lb	6½ oz

Method: Combine ingredients. Mix together for ten minutes until dough becomes stretchy. After mixing dough place in an oiled pot or bowl and allow dough to rise for approximately one hour.

Yield: Seven 12-oz pizzas.

PIZZA SAUCE

Italian plum tomatoes	2 No. 3 Cans
Tomato puree	½ No. 3 Can
Garlic, chopped fine	¼ clove
Salt (to taste)	
Tabasco	¾ teaspoon
Oregano	¾ teaspoon

Method: Put the Italian plum tomatoes through a food grinder with a medium cutter. Combine all ingredients and stir together.

Yield: Sauce for 12 pizzas.

Directions for making pizza

1. After dough has fermented, scale dough into 12-oz pieces or any desired weight.
2. Knead and shape dough pieces into round balls and set aside to proof for at least 30 minutes. (Cover with a dry cloth during this period.)
3. Spread these dough pieces by hand into mounds of 14- to 16-inch diameter. Stretch from the center to outer edges.
4. Over these rounds of dough that have been prepared, spread tomato sauce and sprinkle with grated cheese. Then spread some olive oil over entire top of pizza.
5. Place in a very hot oven 500° to 550°F and bake for 10 to 12 minutes.

Variations: Anchovies, onions, mozzarella cheese, chicken, sliced sausage, mushrooms, and bacon are popular. These toppings go over the sauce and not directly on the dough.

*Yeast may vary according to length of fermentation desired.

BRAN MUFFINS

Sugar	1 lb	
Shortening		8 oz
Salt		½ oz
Eggs	1 lb	
Milk (1½ pints)	1 lb	8 oz
Bran		8 oz
Bread flour	1 lb	8 oz
Baking powder		1½ oz
Honey and molasses		8 oz
	6 lb	10 oz

Method: Cream together sugar, shortening, and salt. Stir in, one after the other, eggs, milk, and bran. Sift together flour and baking powder and mix into batter until smooth. Add honey and molasses to the mixture.

Scaling Instructions: 1⅓ lb per dozen. Yield: Approximately 4 dozen.
Baking instructions: 425°F.

Variation: 1 lb of raisins may be added to this mixture to make raisin bran muffins.

HONEY GLAZE FOR DOUGHNUTS

Confectioner's sugar	10 lb	
Honey		8 oz
Salt		½ oz
Vanilla (to taste)		
Water (1 1/8 qt)	2 lb	4 oz
Gelatin		¾ oz
	12 lb	13¼ oz

Method: Heat water and gelatin to 160°F and mix with other ingredients until smooth. Dip doughnuts into glaze while they are hot.

COFFEE CAKE TOPPINGS AND FILLINGS

CINNAMON SUGAR

Sugar	1 lb	
Cinnamon (variable)		½ oz

Method: Blend together. Sprinkle over top of cake.

DATE FILLING

Dates, ground	2 lb	
Brown sugar		8 oz
Water (1 pint)	1 lb	

Method: Soak dates in water used in filling for 1 hour before grinding. Boil and stir for 10 minutes. Cool before using.

Date and nut: Add 8 oz of chopped nuts to the above mixture.

MELTAWAY FILLING

Confectioner's sugar	2 lb	
Butter and shortening	1 lb	
Milk solids		1 oz
Egg whites		2 oz

Method: Cream together sugar, shortening, and milk solids. Add egg whites and cream lightly.

STREUSEL

Butter and shortening	1 lb
Sugar	1 lb
Cake and bread flour	2 lb
Mace or cinnamon flavor (to taste)	

Method: Rub together until as crumbly as desired.

Variation: Add 4 oz of chopped almonds.

ALMOND FILLING

Almond paste	1 lb	
Sugar	1 lb	
Butter and shortening		8 oz
Pastry flour		4 oz
Eggs		4 oz

Method: Mix almond paste and sugar. Blend flour and shortening and add to first mixture, beating until smooth. Add eggs and blend until smooth.

Cherry Almond filling: Add 8 oz chopped glace cherries to above.
Chocolate Almond filling: Add 4 oz chocolate instead of pastry flour.

CHEESE FILLING

Baker's cheese	1 lb	
Sugar		4 oz
Salt		¼ oz
Eggs, 2		3 oz
Butter, melted		2 oz

Method: Mix all together. Spread over pastry.

Pineapple Cheese: Add 4 oz crushed pineapple.

PEANUT BUTTER FILLING

Brown sugar	12 oz
Peanut butter	12 oz
Salt	½ oz
Butter	12 oz
Cake crumbs, toasted	12 oz
Eggs	4 oz
Water	12 oz

Method: Mix all ingredients together thoroughly.

POPPY SEED FILLING

Poppy seeds	1 lb	
Water		8 oz
Honey		2 oz
Sugar		8 oz
Butter		4 oz
Lemon rind (from 1 lemon)		¼ oz
Cake crumbs	1 lb	
Salt		¼ oz
Eggs		3 oz

Method: Soak poppy seeds in water for 8 hours and grind fine. Add remaining ingredients.

HONEY PAN GLAZE

Brown Sugar	2 lb	
Butter and shortening	1 lb	
Malt		8 oz
Honey		8 oz
Water		4 oz

Method: Cream together all ingredients.

SHINY GLAZE FOR COFFEE CAKE AND DANISH

Corn syrup	3 lb
Water (1 pint)	1 lb

Method: Boil together and apply while hot.

ICING FOR COFFEE CAKE AND DANISH

Confectioner's sugar	5 lb	
Corn syrup		4 oz
Hot water (variable)		10 oz
Egg whites		1 oz
Vanilla or lemon flavoring (to taste)		

Method: Mix all ingredients together thoroughly.

3

Cakes

If uniform results are to be obtained in cake making, the careful weighing of ingredients is absolutely essential. Every bake shop must have a good scale that will weigh from fractions of ounces up to several pounds. This is particularly necessary for leavening agents and flavorings. Accurate scaling prevents fluctuations in the quality of the products from day to day.

MIXING CAKE BATTERS

Extreme care must be taken in the handling and mixing of cake batter. Each type of cake batter should be mixed in accordance with a specific formula. Every phase of the mixing method must be carefully observed.

The three principal ways to mix cake batters are the creaming method, the two-stage method, and the sponge or foam method.

Creaming Method

1. Weigh all ingredients carefully and keep all of them at room temperature.
2. Sugar, shortening or butter, salt, flavors, and spices are usually creamed together.
3. Add required amount of eggs gradually in small amounts, and continue to cream.
4. Add liquids (milk or water as directed) very gradually. In some batters, it is advisable to add only a portion of the liquid alternately with the flour.
5. Add sifted baking powder and flour and mix until a smooth batter is obtained.
6. Throughout the entire mixing process, the sides of the bowl should be scraped down occasionally to ensure a uniform batter.

45

Two-stage Method

1. Weigh all ingredients carefully and keep all of them at room temperature.
2. Place all dry ingredients in a mixing bowl—flour, sugar, spices, baking powder, salt, and any other dry ingredients. Add the shortening and part of the milk and mix at a slow speed for the required amount of time.
3. Add the required amount of eggs to the balance of the milk. Beat slightly and add this to the above mixture in about three parts, scraping the sides of the bowl at intervals.

Sponge or Foam Method

1. Scale all ingredients carefully. All should be at room temperature.
2. Warm eggs and sugar to about 100°F. This dissolves the sugar. Beat until the required temperature is reached.
3. Fold in flour to ensure uniformity.

There are variations to these basic methods. Every formula for cake making should include complete mixing methods.

HIGH-ALTITUDE CAKE BAKING

Almost all formulas released for general distribution to the baking industry are developed in cities at low altitude. The various ingredients in the formulas are balanced with each other so that they produce the desired results at or near sea level. It is recognized, however, that at high altitudes (because of lessened atmospheric pressure) the same formulas must be adjusted to perform satisfactorily.

Those who have baked at higher altitudes have usually followed adjustments worked out through experience on the basis of the older, lower sugar formulas. Generally, these changes for batter cakes consist of reducing the baking powder and sugar, and increasing the liquid as the altitude increases. Such an adjustment protected the physical character of the cakes, but necessarily lowered their eating quality and flavor. As mentioned before, cakes are sweet desserts, and anything that markedly lowers their sweetness detracts from their general appeal and acceptability.

General Mills has carried out extensive work on cake baking at higher altitudes. The results of these tests indicate that with the emulsifier type of shortening and softer cake batters, it is not necessary at higher altitudes to reduce the sugar percentage from sea-level amounts if the sugar percentage ranges from approximately 120-130%, based on flour. This is particularly true in cakes made by the two-stage method, where by standardized shop manipulation, it is possible to control to a large degree the amount of air incorporated in the batter.

It is to be expected that some experimental baking will have to be done to adapt a sea-level formula to the particular elevation of any individual shop and to meet the local conditions that may prevail. The chart on "The Relationship of Altitude to the Amount of Essential Ingredients Used in Cakes" is offered as a guide toward minimizing this unavoidable experimentation.

Relationship of Altitude to the Amount of Essential Ingredients Used In Cakes

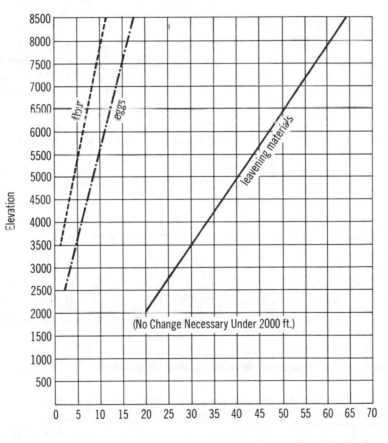

Percent-change in Essential Ingredients From Amounts Used at Sea Level

Because of the lowering of atmospheric pressure as altitude increases and the tremendous effect it has on cake baking, we find that the three ingredients which require adjustment to compensate for this condition are leavening materials, eggs, and flour.

Leavening materials. Reduce baking powder, soda, cream of tartar, or other agents having leavening action in the cakes, beginning at 2000 feet elevation (making a 15% reduction at this elevation), and increase the reduction as the altitude increases, until at 8000 feet elevation the reduction amounts to 60% of the quantity used at sea-level. For example, if a cake formula developed at sea-level calls for 5 oz of baking powder, at 8000 feet elevation only 2 oz should be used.

If a dark cake formula at sea level calls for soda, buttermilk, and/or baking powder, the correction of the leavening agents can best be controlled and adjusted by changing to sweet milk and baking powder only. This eliminates the compensations involved in considering more than one gas-producing leavening ingredient.

It is also suggested that the creaming of the shortening and sugar be standardized both as to machine speed and time so that the volume of air incorporated into the batter will be as uniform as possible. In this manner the volume of the cakes can be controlled and their rapid drying or crumbling can be materially lessened.

Eggs. Beginning at 2500 feet elevation, add 2½% more whole eggs or egg whites. Gradually increase the egg content as the elevation increases, until at 7500 feet 15% more is used. For example, if a formula developed at sea level specified 2 lb 8 oz whole eggs (40 oz), at 2500 feet elevation use 1 oz more, or 2 lb 9 oz. At 7500 feet elevation use a total of 2 lb 14 oz. By increasing the eggs, more liquid is added to the mix and at the same time greater stability is provided, due to the strengthening action of the egg protein.

Flour. Beginning at 3500 feet elevation, increase the flour 2½% and gradually add more as the elevation increases until at 8000 feet elevation 10% more flour is used. For example, if a formula developed at sea-level specifies 5 pounds of Softa-silk cake flour (80 oz), use 2 oz more at 3500 feet elevation, making the total 5 lb 2 oz. This amount should be increased as the elevation increases until at 8000 feet elevation 5 lb 8 oz are used.

As mentioned previously, these corrections or adjustments apply particularly to formulas in which the sugar ranges from 120-130%, based on flour. In addition, the following recommendations are made for cake baking at altitudes of 4500 feet or over:

1. Grease and dust the cake tins somewhat more thoroughly and heavily, as cakes have a tendency to stick to the sides and bottom of the pans.
2. Beginning at 3500 feet elevation increase the oven temperature approximately 25°F. Keep the baking time the same as for sea-level. Precautions should be taken to prevent overbaking because at higher altitudes evaporation takes place much more rapidly and this will contribute to excess dryness in the baked cake.

3. In formulas specifying either whole eggs, egg whites, or egg yolks, make the altitude adjustments as shown on the chart by adding either whole eggs or egg whites. This is recommended to get the benefit of both the egg substance and the extra liquid, which of course is greater in either whole eggs or whites than in the yolks.

4. Less beating of the eggs is required for sponge and angel food cakes, and the acid ingredient (cream of tartar) in the formula should be reduced in the same ratio as for baking powder, as shown in the chart.

5. Maximum moisture and freshness in the baked cakes can be assured if they are removed from the baking tins as soon as they are taken from the oven. Do not cool freshly baked cakes in a strong current of air. Ice them as soon as possible after they are thoroughly cooled.*

Scaling Weights per Cake

Size of Unit	Unit	Scaling Weight	
6 inches	Layer		12 oz
7 inches	Layer	1 lb	
8 inches	Layer	1 lb	8 oz
10 inches	Layer	2 lb	
12 inches	Layer	3 lb	
14 inches	Layer	4 lb	
2¼ × 2½ × 8 inches	Loaf		14 oz
17 × 24 inches	Sheet	5 to 6 lb	
8 inches	Angel		13 oz
2¼ × 2½ × 8 inches	Pound loaf	1 lb	4 oz
12 oz a dozen	Cupcakes		1 oz each

Note: For American sponge cake, scale all cakes 25% lighter than the above weights.

Cake Formula Conversion Table

Liquids

Water	8 oz = 1 cup
Milk	8½ oz = 1 cup
Cream	8-3/8 oz = 1 cup
Sweetened condensed milk	10¼ oz = 1 cup

*This data reprinted from the booklet, "Quality Cakes," by permission of General Mills, Inc., copyright owners.

Flours and Fillers

Cake flour (sifted once)	3-7/8 oz = 1 cup
Bread flour (sifted once)	4¼ oz = 1 cup
Starch (sifted once)	6½ oz = 1 cup
Cake crumbs	3 oz = 1 cup

Sugars

Granulated	7 oz = 1 cup
Confectioner's	5 oz = 1 cup
4X	4½ oz = 1 cup
Brown	7 oz = 1 cup
Fruit fine	7¾ oz = 1 cup
Powdered 6X sifted once	4 oz = 1 cup

Leavenings

Baking powder (cream of tartar type)	1/8 oz = 1 teaspoonful
Baking powder (phosphate—S.A.S. type)	1/6 oz = 1 teaspoonful
Cream of tartar	1/8 oz = 1 teaspoonful
Baking soda	1/6 oz = 1 teaspoonful

Flavors

Flavoring extracts	¾ oz = 6 teaspoonfuls
Cloves, ground	½ oz = 6 teaspoonfuls
Cinnamon, ground	½ oz = 6 teaspoonfuls
Ginger, ground	½ oz = 6 teaspoonfuls
Mace, ground	½ oz = 6 teaspoonfuls
Salt	1 oz = 6 teaspoonfuls
Rind, grated	¾ oz = 6 teaspoonfuls
Caraway seeds, ground	½ oz = 6 teaspoonfuls

Shortening

Butter	7¾ oz = 1 cup
Hydrogenated shortening	6¾ oz = 1 cup

Syrups

Honey	12 oz = 1 cup
Molasses	11 oz = 1 cup

Eggs

Whole (approximately)	5 = 1 cup
Whites (approximately)	8 = 1 cup
Yolks (approximately)	12 = 1 cup

Fruit and Nuts

Coconut, shredded	3½ oz = 1 cup
Coconut, ground	2½ oz = 1 cup
Nuts, pieces	4 oz = 1 cup
Nuts, ground	4¼ oz = 1 cup
Applesauce	8 oz = 1 cup
Currants	4¾ oz = 1 cup
Raisins	4½ oz = 1 cup

Miscellaneous

Candied peel	4 oz = 1 cup
Cottage cheese	7 oz = 1 cup
Chocolate, scraped	3¾ oz = 1 cup
Chocolate, melted	8½ oz = 1 cup
Cocoa	3½ oz = 1 cup
Gelatin	5½ oz = 1 cup

BUTTER RUM CAKE

Sugar	3 lb	8 oz
Butter	2 lb	
Salt		1 oz
Vanilla (to taste)		
Eggs	3 lb	
Milk (1½ pint)	1 lb	8 oz
Cake flour	3 lb	
Baking powder		1½ oz
	13 lb	2½ oz

Method: Creaming. Hold 8 oz of milk and add last.

Scaling instructions: 1 lb to a 6-inch ring.

Baking instructions: 375°F.

Syrup: After baking, remove from pan, cool, and dip in the following rum syrup: Boil together 5 lb of sugar, 1 lb of corn syrup, 1 qt of water, and ½ oz of cream of tartar. Add rum flavor to taste.

Cake Ingredients and Their Functions

Ingredients	Binding agent	Absorbing agent	Aids keeping qualities	Affects eating qualities	Nutritional value	Affects flavor	Adds sweetness	Produces tenderness	Affects symmetry	Imparts crust color	Shortness or tenderness	Eating qualities	Color	Volume	Structure	Grain and Texture	Adds quality to product	Brings out flavor
Cake flour	X	X	X	X	X	X												
Sugar			X		X		X	X	X	X			X					
Shortening & butter			X		X	X					X	X					X	
Salt						X												X
Eggs whole—yolks					X													
Egg whites														X	X	X		
Flavor & spices									X									X
Leavening agent														X		X		
Milk			X		X											X	X	X

Ordinary Cake Faults and Their Causes

Faults	Improper mixing	Batter too stiff	Too much leavening agent	Not enough leavening agent	Batter too slack	Too much heat	Not enough heat	Excessive sugar	Not enough sugar	Improper type of flour	Too much flour	Not enough flour	Cakes scaled too light	Aged baking powder	Over-baking	Under-baking	Sugar too coarse	Not enough eggs	Fruit not drained properly	Not enough shortening	Unbalanced formula	Batter too warm	Not enough liquid
(External)																							
Crust too dark						X		X															
Cakes too small		X		X		X				X			X	X							X	X	
Specks on cake																	X						
Shrinkage of cakes	X				X										X								X
Cake falls during baking												X				X							
Cakes burst on top	X					X				X	X												
Crust too thick							X																
(Internal)																							
Coarse and irregular grain	X	X					X											X			X		
Dense grain				X	X					X											X		
Poor flavor			X								X										X		
Cake tough	X								X	X										X			X
Lack of body in quality			X						X									X					
Sinking of fruit					X					X									X		X		
Poor keeping qualities									X									X		X	X		

BASIC WHITE CAKE

Sugar	2 lb	8 oz
Cake flour	2 lb	8 oz
Salt		1 oz
Baking powder		2 oz
Vanilla or lemon flavoring (to taste)		
Emulsified shortening	1 lb	4 oz
Skim milk (1½ pint)	1 lb	8 oz
Egg whites	1 lb	8 oz
	9 lb	7 oz

Method: Two-stage. Hold 8 oz of milk and the egg whites for second stage. Ice with butter cream, chocolate icing, marshmallow icing, etc.
Scaling instructions: See chart.
Baking instructions: 375°F.

LIGHT FRUITCAKE

Raisins	3 lb	
Mixed diced fruit	3 lb	
Cherries	1 lb	
Orange peel	1 lb	
Lemon peel	1 lb	
Citron	1 lb	
Honey		13 oz
Salt		3 oz
Ginger		¼ oz
Cloves		¼ oz
Cinnamon		¼ oz
Sherry wine (2 qt)	4 lb	
Sugar	3 lb	5 oz
Butter and shortening	2 lb	6 oz
Eggs	1 lb	12 oz
Bread flour	4 lb	2 oz
Walnuts	1 lb	12 oz
	28 lb	5¾ oz

Method: Soak fruits, peels, and citron overnight in the mixture of honey, salt, spices, and wine. To make the batter, cream together sugar and shortening, cream in eggs, and mix in flour until batter is smooth. Add fruits and walnuts. This mixture may be used for Christmas cake or Wedding cake.
Baking instructions: 300°-350°F according to size of cake.

ROMAN APPLE CAKE

Sugar	2 lb	8 oz
Shortening and butter		12 oz
Salt		½ oz
Mace		1/8 oz
Cinnamon		1/8 oz
Eggs		8 oz
Skim milk (1 pint)	1 lb	
Soda		1 oz
Cake flour	2 lb	10 oz
Baking powder		1 oz
Apples, chopped	3 lb	
	10 lb	8¾ oz

Method: Creaming. Add apples and mix in well.
Scaling instructions: 1 lb per 8-inch cake.
Baking instructions: 375°F.

Topping: Butter 8 oz of pecan nuts with 4 oz of melted butter. Sprinkle nuts over the cake batter and sprinkle cinnamon-sugar mixture over the tops of cakes before baking.

DATE AND NUT CAKE

Cake flour	2 lb	8 oz
Sugar	3 lb	
Salt		1½ oz
Soda		½ oz
Baking powder		½ oz
Mace		1/8 oz
Shortening, emulsified	1 lb	4 oz
Buttermilk (1¼ pint)	1 lb	4 oz
Buttermilk (1¾ pint)	1 lb	12 oz
Eggs	1 lb	8 oz
Nuts	1 lb	
Dates, ground	3 lb	
	15 lb	6-5/8 oz

Method: Two-stage. Add nuts and dates and mix. Ice, preferably with chocolate icing.
Scaling instructions: See chart of scaling weights.
Baking instructions: 375°F.

AMERICAN SPONGE CAKE

Sugar	6 lb	
Eggs, whole	4 lb	8 oz
Yolks		8 oz
Vanilla or lemon (to taste)		
Salt		1 oz
Milk (1¼ qt)	2 lb	8 oz
Butter		8 oz
Cake flour	4 lb	8 oz
Baking powder		2 oz
	18 lb	11 oz

Method: Heat sugar in a sheet pan. Combine eggs, yolks, salt, and flavoring, and add sugar. Beat to a lemon color, approximately 10 minutes at high speed. Heat milk and butter until butter is melted. Sift flour and baking powder together and blend. Fold into first mixture alternately with milk.

Scaling instructions: See chart of scaling weights.

Baking instructions: 375°F.

Variations: Layer cakes; Boston cream pie; Washington cream pie; Ice Cream cake; Jelly rolls; Mary Ann cups.

STRAWBERRY LAYER CAKE

Cake flour	3 lb	
Sugar	3 lb	
Salt		1½ oz
Baking powder		1½ oz
Emulsified shortening	1 lb	4 oz
Skim milk (1 pint)	1 lb	
Eggs	2 lb	
Skim milk (1 pint)	1 lb	
Strawberry paste	1 lb	8 oz
	12 lb	15 oz

Method: Two-stage. Add strawberry paste and mix. Ice with strawberry icing.

Scaling instructions: See chart of scaling weights.

Baking instructions: 375°F.

Strawberry Paste: Bring to a boil 2 lb of strawberries and 1 lb of sugar. Cool before using.

Border designs for cake decoration.

ORANGE AND PINEAPPLE CAKE

Cake flour	1 lb	4 oz
Sugar	1 lb	6 oz
Baking powder		¾ oz
Baking soda		1/8 oz
Salt		½ oz
Shortening, Hi-ratio		8 oz
Skim milk		8 oz
Eggs		10 oz
Skim milk		8 oz
Orange and pineapple paste		10 oz
	5 lb	7 3/8 oz

Method: Two-stage. Add and mix paste in well.
Scaling instructions: See chart of scaling weights.
Baking instructions: 375°F.

Orange and pineapple paste: Bring to a boil 3 lb of ground oranges, 2 lb of pineapple, and 1 lb of sugar. Cool before using. This mixture may be used for pineapple cake, using pineapple paste, or for orange cake, using orange paste. Part of the paste may be used for the filling between layers.

FLUFFY CHEESE CAKE

Baker's cheese	4 lb	
Cake flour		4 oz
Cornstarch		8 oz
Salt		2 oz
Vanilla (to taste)		
Soft butter		8 oz
Eggs	2 lb	
Milk (1 pint)	1 lb	
Egg whites	1 lb	8 oz
Cream of tartar		½ oz
Sugar	2 lb	
Water (½ pint)		8 oz
	12 lb	6½ oz

Method: Mix cheese, flour, cornstarch, salt, vanilla, and butter until smooth. Blend eggs and butter, add, and mix until smooth. Beat egg whites until stiff, as for meringue. Boil sugar, water, and cream of tartar to 240°F. Add to beaten whites and make into a stiff meringue. Then fold into cheese mixture.

Baking instructions: 300°F. Grease cake pans and sprinkle with cake crumbs. Fill with the above mixture about seven-eighths full.

CHEESE CAKE

Baker's cheese or cream cheese	2 lb	8 oz
Sugar	1 lb	4 oz
Salt		¼ oz
Milk solids		3 oz
Bread flour		1½ oz
Shortening, emulsified		8 oz
Eggs, whole		8 oz
Yolks		4 oz
Water (1 pint)	1 lb	
	6 lb	4¾ oz

Method: Mix until smooth cheese, sugar, salt, milk solids, and bread flour. Add shortening, eggs, and yolks, and mix until smooth. Add water; the amount will vary according to the dryness of the cheese.

Scaling instructions: 2 lb per 8-inch cake.

Baking instructions: 350°F. Line 8-inch cakepans with sugar cookie dough. Fill pans full with above mixture. Dust lightly with powdered cinnamon. Pie filling, such as cherry or pineapple, may be used on the bottom of the pan before placing cheese filling in the pan. Bake until filling is set. Take care not to overbake.

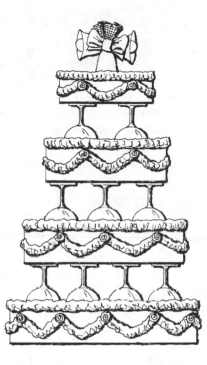

Tiered wedding cake with champagne glass dividers.

BRIDE'S CAKE

Sugar	4 lb	
Butter and shortening	1 lb	2 oz
Vanilla (to taste)		
Salt		1 oz
Egg whites	2 lb	
Milk	3 lb	
Cake flour	4 lb	
Baking powder		2 oz
	14 lb	5 oz

Method: Creaming.
Baking instructions: Fill pans two-thirds full and bake at 325°F.

MACAROON CUPCAKES

Egg whites	2 lb	
Salt		½ oz
Vanilla (to taste)		
Cream of tartar		¼ oz
Sugar	1 lb	8 oz

Sugar	2 lb	
Cake flour		3 oz
Macaroon coconut	2 lb	8 oz
	8 lb	3¾ oz

Method: Whip egg whites, salt, and vanilla until foamy. Add sugar and cream of tartar and continue to whip until whites peak. Blend sugar, flour, and coconut and fold into mixture.
Scaling instructions: 8 dozen cupcakes.
Baking instructions: Fill cupcake forms seven-eighths full and bake at 375°F.

DEVIL FUDGE CAKE

Cake flour	2 lb	
Cocoa		8 oz
Sugar	3 lb	8 oz
Salt		1½ oz
Baking powder		1½ oz
Cinnamon		1/8 oz
Baking soda		½ oz
Shortening, emulsified	1 lb	
Skim milk (1¼ pint)	1 lb	4 oz
Skim milk (1½ pint)	1 lb	8 oz
Eggs	1 lb	8 oz
	11 lb	7-5/8 oz

Method: Two-stage. Ice with Devil Fudge icing.
Scaling instructions: See chart of scaling weights.
Baking instructions: 375°F.

BANANA CAKE

Cake flour	2 lb	8 oz
Sugar	3 lb	
Salt		1½ oz
Baking powder		1½ oz
Baking soda		½ oz
Shortening, emulsified	1 lb	
Bananas, ripe	2 lb	
Skim milk (1 pint)	1 lb	
Eggs	2 lb	
Vanilla (to taste)		
	11 lb	11½ oz

Method: Mix dry ingredients, shortening, bananas, and milk 5 to 7 minutes at slow speed. Add eggs and vanilla in three parts, scraping sides of bowl each time, and mix 3 to 5 minutes. Ice with Banana icing.
Scaling instructions: See chart of scaling weights.
Baking instructions: 375°F.

JELLY ROLL SPONGE

Eggs, whole		12 oz
Yolks		6 oz
Sugar	1 lb	8 oz
Salt		½ oz
Vanilla or lemon (to taste)		
Milk powder		1½ oz
Water		12 oz
Honey		3 oz
Cake flour	1 lb	5 oz
Baking powder		½ oz
	5 lb	½ oz

Method: Beat eggs, yolks, sugar, salt, vanilla, and milk powder for approximately 10 minutes at high speed until the mixture becomes lemon-colored. Heat honey and water and add to first mixture. Sift together flour and baking powder and fold in.
Scaling instructions: Line two 18 X 24-inch sheet pans with paper, and divide dough between them.
Baking instructions: 375°F.

Variations: Jelly roll; Lemon roll; Mocha roll; Marshmallow roll; Ice Cream roll.
Chocolate Roll: Use 1 lb of cake flour, 5 oz of cocoa, and ½ oz of baking soda. Proceed the same way.

FRENCH COFFEE CAKE

Sugar	2 lb	4 oz
Shortening and butter	1 lb	2 oz
Salt		½ oz
Vanilla (to taste)		
Eggs	1 lb	8 oz
Milk (1 qt)	2 lb	
Cake flour	3 lb	
Baking powder		1½ oz
	10 lb	

Method: Creaming. Top cake with streusel before baking. After baking cool and
cut into 2-in. squares and serve.
Scaling instructions: 18 × 24 × 1-in. sheet pans.
Baking instructions: 375°F.

YELLOW CAKE, BASIC

Cake flour	5 lb	
Sugar	5 lb	
Salt		3 oz
Baking powder		3¾ oz
Shortening, emulsified	2 lb	6 oz
Skim milk (1 qt)	2 lb	
Eggs	2 lb	8 oz
Skim milk (1½ pint)	1 lb	8 oz
Vanilla (to taste)		
	18 lb	12¾ oz

Method: Two-stage.
Scaling instructions: See chart of scaling weights.
Baking instructions: 350°-375°F.

Variations: Sheet cake; Loaf cake; Cupcakes; Layer cakes.

CHOCOLATE CAKE

Sugar	2 lb	8 oz
Shortening and butter	1 lb	
Cake flour	2 lb	
Salt		¾ oz
Baking powder		¾ oz
Baking soda		¼ oz
Vanilla (to taste)		
Bitter chocolate, melted		8 oz
Skim milk (1¼ pint)	1 lb	4 oz
Eggs	1 lb	4 oz
Skim milk (¾ pint)		12 oz
	9 lb	5¾ oz

Method: Two-stage. Ice with Chocolate icing.
Scaling instructions: See chart of scaling weights.
Baking instructions: 375°F.

APPLE SAUCE CAKE

Cake flour	2 lb	8 oz
Sugar	2 lb	8 oz
Baking powder		1 oz
Baking soda		½ oz
Cinnamon		¼ oz
Cloves		¼ oz
Salt		1½ oz
Shortening, emulsified	1 lb	
Apple sauce	3 lb	
Eggs		12 oz
Raisins	1 lb	8 oz
	11 lb	7½ oz

Method: Mix together for 5 to 7 minutes at slow speed flour, sugar, baking soda, baking powder, spices, salt, shortening, and half of the apple sauce. Add eggs. Add remaining apple sauce and raisins, scraping sides of bowl. Mix 3 to 5 minutes at slow speed. Add raisins last. Ice with Lemon icing.

Scaling instructions: See chart of scaling weights.
Baking instructions: 375°F.

GINGERBREAD CAKE

Sugar	2 lb	8 oz
Shortening, Hi-ratio	1 lb	4 oz
Eggs	1 lb	4 oz
Molasses	4 lb	
Cake flour	5 lb	
Baking soda		3½ oz
Cinnamon		1 oz
Ginger		1 oz
Salt		2 oz
Skim milk (2 qt)	4 lb	
	18 lb	7½ oz

Method: Cream sugar and shortening. Add eggs and cream. Stir in molasses. Sift and blend together dry ingredients, add milk, and mix smooth.

Scaling instructions: See chart of scaling weights.
Baking instructions: 360°-375°F.

Variations: Layer cakes; Sheet cakes; Mary Ann cups.

ANGEL FOOD CAKE

Egg whites	2 lb	
Vanilla (to taste)		
Sugar	1 lb	
Cream of tartar		¼ oz
Salt		¼ oz
Sugar	1 lb	
Cake flour		13 oz
	4 lb	13½ oz

Method: Beat egg whites and vanilla at high speed for 5 minutes. Blend sugar, cream of tartar, and slowly add egg whites, beating until they form a wet peak. Sift flour and blend with sugar, add, and fold in. Precautions should be taken not to overbeat this mixture and to fold in flour and sugar only after whites are thoroughly mixed. Otherwise, the cakes will collapse and the volume will be smaller.

Baking instructions: 350°F. Turn the cake upside down after removing from the oven. Allow to cool before removing from pans.

YELLOW POUND CAKE

Cake flour	5 lb	
Sugar	5 lb	
Baking powder		1 oz
Salt		2 oz
Nutmeg		¼ oz
Shortening, emulsified	2 lb	
Butter	1 lb	
Skim milk (1 qt)	2 lb	
Eggs	3 lb	
Milk (1 pint)	1 lb	
Vanilla (to taste)		
	19 lb	3¼ oz

Method: Two-stage.
Scaling instructions: See chart of scaling weights.
Baking instructions: 350°F.

Variations: Raisin pound cake; Nut fudge cake; Marble pound cake.

SHEET CAKES

The simplest form of pastry dessert that can be made is the sheet cake. It is simple because it can be made from a variety of baking mixes, all of them available from a food wholesaler. On the package of these mixes are simple, one-two-three steps for mixing and baking sheet cakes. The sheet cake can also be made from a recipe. In either case, the sheet cake becomes a base that offers a variety of opportunities. It is not only easy to make, but also easy to decorate to fit any occasion.

For instance, in school lunch programs, the sheet cake can be used as a good, plain, and inexpensive food, or it can be frosted and trimmed to delight youngsters. In a restaurant, the same sheet cake becomes the basis of tiny decorative petit fours. Variations run from the plain and simple to the formal and extra fancy desserts. The variety comes in the trim.

One of the many advantages of the sheet cake is its ability to stay fresh. Baked as one large unit, the sheet cake retains its moisture and freshness much longer than many smaller units that are more fully exposed to the air and therefore more readily dry out.

This staying quality is especially important. It offers volume feeders an opportunity to take advantage of slack kitchen time and use it creatively and profitably. The cakes can be baked ahead and stored. This also guarantees not getting caught short when the need for pastry and cake arises unexpectedly.

CUTTING CAKES

There is a satisfactory method of cutting each kind of cake. The factors to keep in mind are the size and number of servings and the cutting utensil to be used. The size and number of servings depend upon the size and number of layers in the cake. A knife with a sharp straight-edged, thin blade is most suitable for cutting batter cakes. To make a clean cut, dip the blade into warm water before cutting each portion and keep the blade free from frosting and cake crumbs.

Fruit cake, which also is a batter type cake, may be cut in the same manner. Because of its richness, fruit cake servings generally are smaller than those shown for layer cakes.

The accompanying diagrams illustrate methods of cutting cakes of various sizes and shapes. The average number of servings per cake are given.

Sheet Cake Cutting Chart

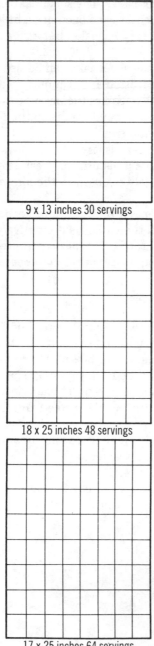

9 x 13 inches 30 servings

18 x 25 inches 48 servings

17 x 25 inches 64 servings

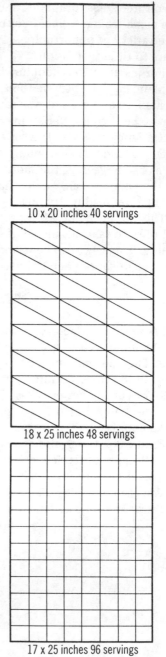

10 x 20 inches 40 servings

18 x 25 inches 48 servings

17 x 25 inches 96 servings

Square Cake Cutting Chart

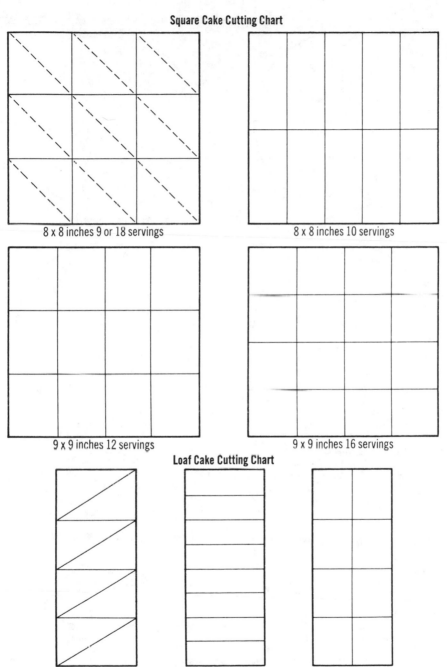

8 x 8 inches 9 or 18 servings

8 x 8 inches 10 servings

9 x 9 inches 12 servings

9 x 9 inches 16 servings

Loaf Cake Cutting Chart

1 pound cakes 8 servings

Two-Layer Cake Cutting Chart

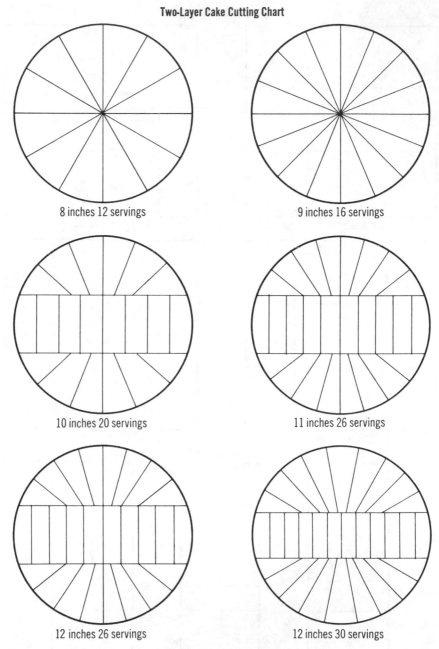

8 inches 12 servings

9 inches 16 servings

10 inches 20 servings

11 inches 26 servings

12 inches 26 servings

12 inches 30 servings

Three-layer cakes should be cut in the same manner as shown above. However, reduce the size of each serving approximately one-third in order to increase the number of servings.

Two-Layer Cake Cutting Chart

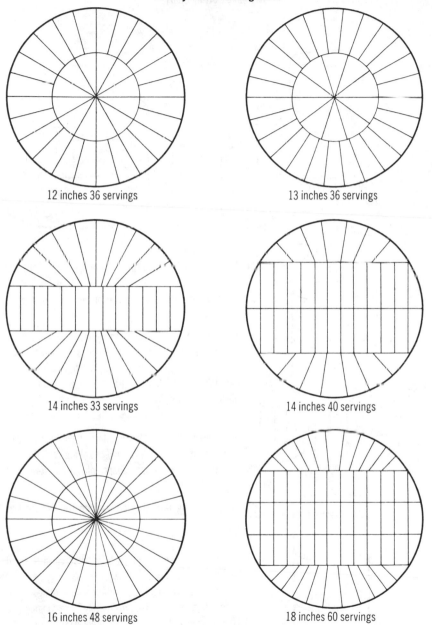

12 inches 36 servings

13 inches 36 servings

14 inches 33 servings

14 inches 40 servings

16 inches 48 servings

18 inches 60 servings

Three-layer cakes should be cut in the same manner as shown above. However, reduce the size of each serving approximately one-third in order to increase the number of servings.

Tier Cake Cutting Chart

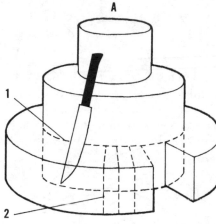

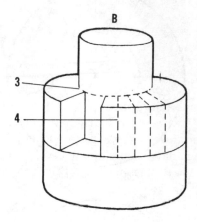

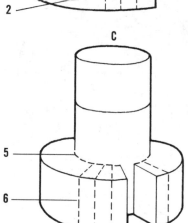

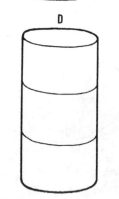

A—Cut vertically through the bottom layer at the edge of the second layer as indicated by the dotted line marked 1; then cut out wedge-shaped pieces as shown by 2.

B—When these pieces have been served, follow the same procedure with the middle layer; cut vertically through the second layer at the edge of the top layer as indicated by dotted line 3; then cut out wedge-shaped pieces as shown by 4.

C—When pieces from the second layer have been served, return to the bottom layer and cut along dotted line 5; cut another row of wedge-shaped pieces as shown by 6.

D—The remaining tiers may be cut into the desired size pieces.

The average number of portions that various sized layers will yield are as follows:

14 inch layer will yield approximately 40 servings.
12 inch layer will yield approximately 30 servings.
10 inch layer will yield approximately 20 servings.
 9 inch layer will yield approximately 16 servings.
 8 inch layer will yield approximately 12 servings.

4

Cookies

Cookies are one of the most profitable items produced by bakers. Important in their production is the use of high grade ingredients. Butter is the preferred shortening. Careful choice of the purest of spices, molasses, and flavorings will assure delicious cookies. Cookies should be baked fresh each day, if possible. When it is necessary to bake a week's output at one time, this can be done if the cookies are properly stored.

MIXING METHODS

There are two basic methods for mixing cookies: the creaming method and the one-stage method.

Creaming Method

1. Place the sugar, butter or shortening, salt, and spices in a mixing bowl and cream together.
2. Add the eggs and liquid.
3. Add the flour and leavening agent last.

One-stage Method

1. Place all ingredients into a mixing bowl and mix until all are smoothly blended.
2. Allow two or three minutes at low speed for mixing.

TYPES OF COOKIES

There are six basic kinds of cookies: rolled, icebox, spritz, bar, sheet, and dropped.

Rolled Method: The dough is easier to handle if chilled first. Roll out 1/8-inch thick on a flour bag. Cut to desired shape and size with a cookie cutter. Place on baking sheets and bake.

Icebox Method: Weigh dough at 1 lb 8 oz and roll into bars 18 inches long. Roll in waxed paper and place rolls on sheet pans. Refrigerate overnight. Slice into ½-inch strips and bake.

71

Ordinary Cookie Faults and Their Causes

Faults	Improper mix	Insufficient sugar	Too much sugar	Flour too strong	Too much flour	Insufficient leavening	Too much leavening	Too much baking soda	Not enough baking soda	Insufficient eggs	Too much shortening	Insufficient shortening	Over-baked	Too low baking temperature	Too high baking temperature	Pan insufficiently greased	Dough too slack	Insufficient liquid	Poor quality ingredients	Unbalanced formula	Cookie pans unclean and uneven
Spreading	X		X					X						X			X				
Crumbly	X		X				X			X	X										
Tough	X	X	X	X	X																
Hard				X								X	X	X				X			
Dry				X	X							X	X	X				X			
Pale in color		X			X		X							X							
Lack of flavor																			X	X	
Sticking to pans	X		X													X				X	X
Sugary crust	X		X				X														X
Lack of spread	X	X		X		X			X						X	X					

Ordinary Cookie Faults and Their Causes

Spritz or Bagged Method: Put mixture into pastry bag with desired size and shaped tube. Press directly onto sheet pans. Garnish with cherries, nuts, etc., and bake.

Bar Method: Scale the dough into 1-lb pieces and roll out to the length of the sheet pan. Place on the sheet pans, leaving a space between the strips. Place three strips on each pan. Flatten with the fingers and shape into uniform 1-inch strips. Apply egg wash and bake.

Sheet Method: Spread the cookie mixture onto sheet pans. Wash with egg or sprinkle with nuts and bake. Cool and cut into squares or oblongs.

Dropped Method: Drop mixture on sheet pans with a spoon. Press or flatten out with a weight or special cookie die. Strips of dough may also be cut into ½-inch pieces. If the dough is rich it will spread by itself. Do not press or flatten.

THE PASTRY BAG

The pastry bag of yesterday was generally made of canvas. Today the pastry bag is made of a specialized material, nonabsorbing, durable, and easy to clean. It has many uses. Its contents may range from mashed potatoes to elegant cream mixtures. Its uses in the kitchen are unlimited: Duchess potatoes, fancy mashed potato borders on various meat, fish, or vegetable platters; fancy cookies; garnishes and toppings of various mixtures; fancy cream toppings. The pastry bag is used to fill pastries; and last but not least, the pastry bag is filled with icings to decorate the simplest or fanciest cakes.

To care for the pastry bag, one fact is very important—it must always be turned inside out and scrubbed very thoroughly after each use, using hot water. This will prevent the bag from becoming sour and stale after being filled with the rich mixtures. Remember to always remove the tube when washing the pastry bag; the tube must also be carefully washed and stored. To dry the pastry bag, hang it up by the loop to enable it to air dry.

The pastry bag comes with various pastry tubes of different shapes and sizes. Select the one you want and insert it into the bag from the inside. To fill the pastry bag, fold back half of the bag and hold it open with the left hand under the fold. Place the mixture into the bag with the right hand, using a spatula or spoon. Fill no more than 2/3 full. Close up the bag and give a slight twist at the top to seal off the mixture and eliminate leakage from the top.

To use the bag, squeeze from the top with the right hand, and guide with the left, leaving the tube visible. When using a stiff mixture, hold the top of the bag closed with the left hand and squeeze the lower section of it with the right hand. This method requires less pressure.

The Pastry Bag

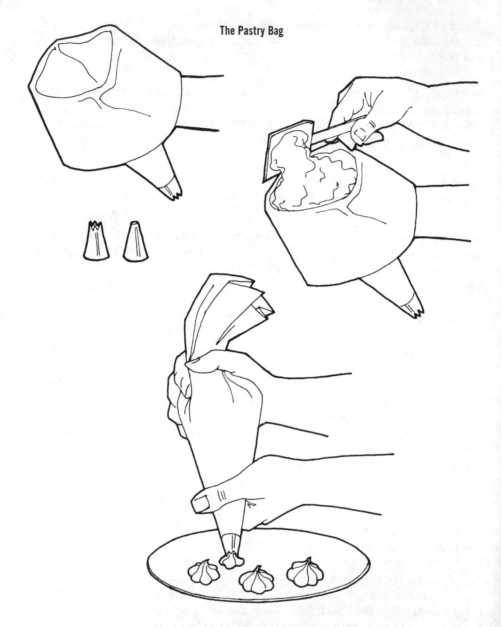

ICEBOX COOKIES *(Yellow Mix)*

Confectioner's sugar	2 lb	
Butter and shortening	2 lb	
Salt		½ oz
Vanilla (to taste)		
Eggs		8 oz
Cake flour	3 lb	
	7 lb	8½ oz

Method: Creaming. Roll into strips about 18 inches long. Roll a piece of waxed paper around each strip. Pack the strips on sheet pans. Place in refrigerator overnight. Remove from refrigerator and slice into ¼-inch slices. A slicing machine may be used to assure uniformity. Place on ungreased pans. Bake lightly, avoiding too much bottom heat.
Scaling instructions: Each strip, 1 lb 8 oz.
Baking instructions: 375°F.

Variations: Fruit or nuts may be added to this mix. Checkerboard and Pinwheels can be made from yellow mix and chocolate mix.

ICEBOX COOKIES *(Butterscotch)*

Brown sugar	1 lb	
Confectioner's sugar	1 lb	
Butter	1 lb	8 oz
Salt		½ oz
Eggs, whole		10 oz
Cake flour	3 lb	
Baking powder		¼ oz
	7 lb	2¾ oz

Method: Follow same instructions as for Icebox Cookies *(Yellow Mix)*.
Baking instructions: 375°F.

ICEBOX COOKIES *(White Mix)*

Confectioner's sugar	2 lb	
Butter and shortening	2 lb	
Salt		½ oz
Almond flavoring (to taste)		
Egg whites		8 oz
Cake flour	2 lb	12 oz
	7 lb	4½ oz

Method: Follow same instructions as for Icebox Cookies *(Yellow Mix)*.

Scaling instructions: 8 oz per roll.
Baking instructions: 375°F.

ICEBOX COOKIES *(Chocolate)*

Confectioner's sugar	1 lb	12 oz
Butter and shortening	1 lb	8 oz
Salt		½ oz
Vanilla (to taste)		
Eggs, whole		12 oz
Milk		4 oz
Soda		1/8 oz
Cake flour	3 lb	
Cocoa		8 oz
	7 lb	12-5/8 oz

Method: Follow same instructions as for Icebox Cookies (*Yellow Mix*).
Baking instructions: 375°F.

CHOCOLATE BROWNIES

Bittersweet chocolate	1 lb	
Butter	1 lb	8 oz
Eggs	1 lb	4 oz
Sugar	3 lb	
Vanilla (to taste)		
Cake flour	1 lb	
Nuts (pecans or walnuts)	1 lb	8 oz
	9 lb	4 oz

Method: Melt chocolate and butter. Beat together eggs, sugar, and vanilla until
lemon colored (about 10 minutes). Add chocolate and butter. Sift
flour and fold into mixture. Add only enough flour to incorporate
well. Fold about 1 lb of nuts into the mixture. Place mixture into
sheet pan. Sprinkle balance of nuts on top of mixture.
Scaling instructions: 9 lb 4 oz per 18 × 24-inch sheet pan. The yield is about
8 doz 2 × 2-inch brownies; cut 8 × 12 to each sheet pan.
Baking instructions: 350°F.

BUTTERSCOTCH BROWNIES

Brown sugar	2 lb	
Butter	1 lb	
Water		4 oz
Eggs	1 lb	

Brown sugar	1 lb	
Vanilla (to taste)		
Baking powder		½ oz
Cake flour	2 lb	
Walnuts	1 lb	8 oz
	8 lb	12½ oz

Method: To make butterscotch mixture, dissolve sugar, butter, and water with
heat. Beat eggs, sugar, and vanilla until lemon colored (about
10 minutes) and add to butterscotch. Sift flour and baking powder
and fold into mixture. Add 1 lb of nuts and mix. Place in an 18 ×
24-inch sheet pan and sprinkle top with 8 oz of chopped nuts.
Scaling instructions: 8 lb 12 oz per 18 × 24-inch sheet pans. Yields about
8 doz 2 × 2-inch brownies. Cut 8 × 12 to each sheet pan.
Baking instructions: 325°F.

FANCY BUTTER COOKIES

Almond paste		8 oz
Powdered sugar	1 lb	8 oz
Eggs	1 lb	
Shortening and butter	2 lb	
Cake flour	3 lb	
	8 lb	

Method: Rub together almond paste and sugar. Add eggs gradually to obtain a
smooth batter. Add shortening and whip until light. Add flour and
mix until smooth. Do not overmix. Then tube out to form various
shapes.
Baking instructions: 375°F.

VANILLA WAFERS

Sugar	1 lb	
Butter and shortening	1 lb	
Salt		¼ oz
Vanilla (to taste)		
Eggs		12 oz
Pastry flour	1 lb	6 oz
	4 lb	2¼ oz

Method: Creaming. Bag out with plain tube on slightly greased pans. Leave
sufficient space between drops for spreading. Bake until the edges
are brown; remove from oven. Avoid overbaking.
Baking instructions: 375°F.

FRENCH MACAROONS

Almond and Macaroon paste	2 lb	
Powdered sugar		12 oz
Granulated sugar		12 oz
Egg whites*		8 oz
	4 lb	

Method: Break up paste and sugars until fine. Gradually add whites until a smooth medium paste is obtained. Bag out with fine star tube on paper-lined pans. Decorate with fruit or nuts, let stand overnight and bake on double pans in a hot oven. Glaze while still hot with a hot mixture of three parts glucose and one part water.
Baking instructions: 400°F.

COCONUT MACAROONS *(Chewy)*

Sugar	1 lb	
Water		4 oz
Glucose		4 oz
Butter		2 oz
Salt		1/8 oz
Vanilla (to taste)		
Macaroon (coconut)	1 lb	
Cake flour		1 oz
Cream of tartar		1/8 oz
Egg whites		6 oz
	3 lb	1¼ oz

Method: Bring sugar, water, glucose, butter, salt, and vanilla to a boil. Remove from heat and mix in rest of ingredients. Bag out with plain tube on paper-lined sheet pans.
Baking instructions: 325°-350°F.

COCONUT MACAROONS *(Light Meringue)*

Sugar	1 lb	
Water		4 oz
Egg whites		8 oz
Granulated sugar		8 oz
Salt		¼ oz
Vanilla (to taste)		
Macaroon (coconut)	1 lb	
	3 lb	4¼ oz

*Egg whites vary depending on the dryness of the paste.

Method: Boil sugar and water to 242°F to make syrup. Whip egg whites and vanilla until light and add sugar until a wet peak is produced. Then add syrup. Bag out on paper-lined pans with star tube.
Baking instructions: 300°F.

ALMOND MACAROONS

Almond paste	2 lb	
Granulated sugar	2 lb	
Egg whites (variable)		10 oz
	4 lb	10 oz

Method: Rub paste and sugar together until fine. Add whites gradually to sugar and paste until smooth. This makes a medium stiff paste. Press out with a plain tube on paper-lined sheet pans. Dampen the macaroons with a towel before baking. Do not permit them to dry before placing in the oven.
Baking instructions: 325°F.

CHOCOLATE CHIP COOKIES

Brown and granulated sugar	1 lb	8 oz
Butter and shortening	1 lb	8 oz
Baking soda		½ oz
Salt		½ oz
Water		1 oz
Vanilla (to taste)		
Eggs		8 oz
Pastry flour	2 lb	4 oz
Chocolate chips	1 lb	
Walnuts, chopped		8 oz
	7 lb	6 oz

Method: Creaming. Bag out with plain tube on slightly greased pans.
Baking instructions: 375°F.

SHORTBREAD COOKIES *(Sables)*

Sugar		14 oz
Butter	1 lb	8 oz
Salt		½ oz
Lemon rind (1 lemon)		
Egg yolks		8 oz
Cake flour	2 lb	
	4 lb	14½ oz

Method: Creaming. Refrigerate for several hours. Roll out about ¼-inch thick and cut into various shapes. Wash and sprinkle with nuts or granulated sugar or decorate with nuts or cherries.
Baking instructions: 350°F.

SHORT PASTE COOKIE DOUGH

Sugar	1 lb	
Shortening and butter	1 lb	8 oz
Salt		½ oz
Eggs		4 oz
Milk		4 oz
Vanilla (to taste)		
Pastry flour	2 lb	8 oz
	5 lb	8½ oz

Method: Creaming. Roll out about one-eighth-inch thick and cut out with cookie cutters into various shapes. Wash and decorate. Bake lightly.
Baking instructions: 375°F.

RAINBOW SLICE COOKIES

Granulated sugar	3 lb	
Shortening and butter	3 lb	
Salt		1 oz
Vanilla (to taste)		
Lemon flavoring (to taste)		
Eggs	4 lb	
Cake flour	4 lb	
Baking powder		1 oz
	14 lb	2 oz

Method: Creaming. Divide entire mixture into 4 equal parts. Color each part separately—green, yellow, pink, and orange. Spread each mixture on paper-lined sheet pans. Bake lightly. When cool, spread jam lightly over cake, sandwiching all 4 colored layers. Press down well with sheet pan, making an even, firm sandwich. Roll out marzipan 1/16-inch thick and place on the upper side of cake. Melt sweet chocolate and spread over marzipan. Allow to set. Reverse sheet, placing marzipan layer on the other side, and spread with melted chocolate. Cut into 1½-inch by ½-inch slices when dry.
Baking instructions: 375°F.

GINGER SNAPS

Brown sugar		12 oz
Shortening	1 lb	
Salt		½ oz
Water		4 oz
Baking soda		½ oz
Molasses (1 pint)	1 lb	2 oz
Pastry flour	2 lb	
Ginger		½ oz
	4 lb	3½ oz

Method: Cream together sugar, salt, and shortening. Dissolve baking soda in water and add to first mixture. Stir in molasses. Sift flour and ginger together and mix with above until smooth. Refrigerate for several hours. Roll out 1/8-inch thick and cut out with cutters.
Baking instructions: 375°F.

Variations: This mixture may also be used for the gingerbread houses and for gingerbread men.

NUT WAFERS—NUT FINGERS

Egg whites	1 lb	
Sugar	1 lb	
Confectioner's sugar	1 lb	
Nuts, finely sifted	1 lb	
Corn starch		2 oz
Cinnamon (to taste)		
	4 lb	2 oz

Method: Beat egg whites and add sugar until a wet peak meringue is secured. Blend remaining ingredients and fold into egg whites. Bag out with a plain tube onto paper-lined pans. Press out round or in finger shapes.
Baking instructions: 275°F.

PEANUT BUTTER COOKIES

Brown and granulated sugar	2 lb	
Shortening	1 lb	
Peanut butter	1 lb	8 oz
Salt		½ oz
Eggs	1 lb	

Milk		4 oz
Baking soda		¼ oz
Pastry flour	2 lb	
Baking powder		¼ oz
	7 lb	13 oz

Method: Cream together sugar, shortening, peanut butter, and salt. Add eggs and cream together. Dissolve baking soda in milk and add. Sift together flour and baking powder, add to mixture, and mix until smooth. Roll into strips, flatten, and wash. After baking, cut out while still warm.

Scaling instructions: 96 cookies.

Baking instructions: 350°F.

SUGAR COOKIES

Sugar	1 lb	
Shortening		12 oz
Salt		½ oz
Eggs		6 oz
Milk		6 oz
Vanilla (to taste)		
Pastry flour	2 lb	
Baking powder		¼ oz
	4 lb	15½ oz

Method: Cream together sugar, shortening, and salt. Add eggs and cream. Stir in milk and vanilla. Sift together flour and baking powder, add to mixture, and mix until smooth. Roll out ¼-inch thick and sprinkle granulated sugar over the surface. Cut out and bake on lightly greased pans.

Baking instructions: 375°F.

BUTTER COOKIES

Sugar	1 lb	
Butter	1 lb	
Salt		¼ oz
Eggs		8 oz
Pastry flour	2 lb	
	4 lb	8 oz

Method: Creaming. Roll out 1/8-inch thick and cut out with various shaped cookie cutters—stars, bells, rabbits, animal figures, etc. Wash, decorate, and bake.

Baking instructions: 375°F.

LADYFINGERS

Egg whites, 16	1 lb	
Sugar	1 lb	
Egg yolks, 16	1 lb	
Bread flour	1 lb	
	5 lb	

Method: Gradually add sugar to whites, and beat to a stiff peak. Beat yolks and fold into mixture. Sift flour and fold into mixture. Press into finger shapes with a plain tube on paper-lined sheet pans. Dust with powdered sugar and bake immediately.

Baking instructions: 400°F.

OATMEAL COOKIES

Sugar	1 lb	
Shortening		8 oz
Salt		½ oz
Malt and molasses		8 oz
Eggs		4 oz
Milk		8 oz
Baking soda		½ oz
Pastry flour	1 lb	4 oz
Baking powder		¾ oz
Oatmeal		12 oz
Raisins	1 lb	
	5 lb	13¾ oz

Method: Cream together salt, sugar, shortening, malt, and molasses. Add eggs. Dissolve baking soda in milk and stir in. Add flour, oatmeal, and raisins, and mix thoroughly. Bag out with a plain tube onto lightly-greased pans.

Baking instructions: 375°F.

MINTS

Sugar	3 lb	
Water (1 pint)	1 lb	
Peppermint flavor (to taste)		
Confectioner's sugar	1 lb	8 oz
	5 lb	8 oz

Method: Cook sugar and water to a soft ball, 238°-240°F. After cooking, add flavoring and confectioner's sugar and mix smooth. Pipe out onto paper, marble slab, or rubber mat.

PETIT FOURS

Petit fours (or, as they are known in America, tea cakes or small fancy cakes), may be classified into two categories: petit fours glacé and petit fours sec.

Petit fours glacé are generally very small (petit) fancy cakes made from various sponges, cake mixtures, and franchipan (see recipe below); sometimes they are left with no filling and sometimes they are filled with jams, icing, cream, or marzipan. They are made in many different shapes and iced or glazed with colored fondant, chocolate, or jellies. Then they are decorated with fancy designs—florals or abstract designs, for instance. Petit fours make for good eating and also have a great deal of eye appeal.

To make petit fours glacé use a firm type of sponge or yellow cake one-half inch in thickness. Remove the sheet cake from the pan and trim off all loose crust. Spread surface with hot apricot jam. Next, cut small dainty squares, oblongs, or diamond shapes and arrange these pieces carefully on the icing screen. Then with your pastry tube filled with prepared butter cream, pipe out an oval bulb of buttercream onto each piece. Place these in the refrigerator to chill thoroughly. Remove them from refrigerator and ice with fondant icing in a variety of colors. When dry, set in paper cases and decorate with appropriate designs.

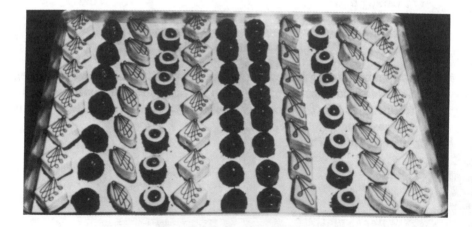

Petit fours glacé.

Petit fours sec (or dry type) are small fancy cakes or cookies made from cookie dough, almond paste, or marzipan and combined with jams, icings, creams, chocolate, and the like. Unlike petit fours glacé, petit fours sec are not coated with fondant. Fancy cookies are also sometimes classified as petit fours sec. It must be remembered that petit fours sec must be made very carefully and patiently for best results.

Petit fours sec.

FRANCHIPAN

Butter		8 oz
Sugar		8 oz
Almond paste	1 lb	
Eggs		4 oz
Eggs		8 oz
Bread flour		5 oz
	3 lb	1 oz

Method: Cream together butter and sugar. Soften almond paste with eggs and add to butter and sugar. Continue to cream this mixture. Add remaining eggs and cream well. Add flour, mix smooth, and pan as required.
Baking instructions: 375°F.

CHINESE ALMOND COOKIES

Cake flour	1 lb	
Sugar		8 oz
Baking soda		¼ oz
Baking powder		¼ oz

Shortening		8 oz
Eggs, whole (2 large)		4 oz
Almond extract (to taste)		
	2 lb	4½ oz

Method: Sift together dry ingredients and blend. Add shortening and mix. Add remaining ingredients and mix. Brush cookies with milk and place a split almond on top.

Scaling instructions: 1 oz per cookie

Baking instructions: 375°F.

CHOCOLATE LEAVES

Almond paste	1 lb	
Confectioner's sugar		12 oz
Bread flour		4 oz
Egg whites		4 oz
Milk (variable)		4 oz
	2 lb	8 oz

Method: Rub together almond paste, sugar, and flour, and blend thoroughly. Add egg whites and mix smooth. Add and mix milk into proper consistency. Bake on greased and floured pans. Cover with melted chocolate after baking and mark to give leaf effect.

Baking instructions: 350°F.

5

Pies

PIE CRUSTS

There are two basic types of pie crusts: flaky pie crust and mealy pie crust. Although they may contain identical ingredients in the same amounts, the results may be quite different.

Flaky crust is made by rubbing the flour and shortening together until they become nuggets the size of walnuts before adding the liquid and salt.

Mealy crust is made by rubbing the flour and shortening together until there is a finer distribution of the shortening through the flour.

Ingredients

Always use a soft wheat flour, such as pastry flour, for pie crusts. If a stronger flour is used, it must be worked with a higher proportion of fat. Shortening used in making pie crusts must be of plastic consistency. Lard is a good choice but many people object to the taste. Vegetable shortening is most popular. A proportion of butter greatly improves the flavor and should be used where the cost factor is not too serious. Water must always be very cold when used for making pie crusts. The salt is usually dissolved in the water.

Thus the essential ingredients that go into the making of a good pie crust are pastry flour, vegetable shortening (with some butter added if possible), salt, and cold water. Some formulas may call for other ingredients such as vinegar or baking powder, but these items do not improve the crust.

One important point: pie dough should never be overmixed.

Pie trimmings. When crusts are being rolled out, care should be taken to keep the size of each piece as near as possible to the size of the pans, thus keeping the size of the trimmings to a minimum. Pie trimmings should be used to make no more than half of a crust and should be used for the bottom crust only.

Pie washes. Milk, cream, eggs and milk, melted butter and water, are the various kinds of pie washes used to improve eye appeal of pie crusts. The wash to be used depends upon the finish required.

Lattice Pie Top

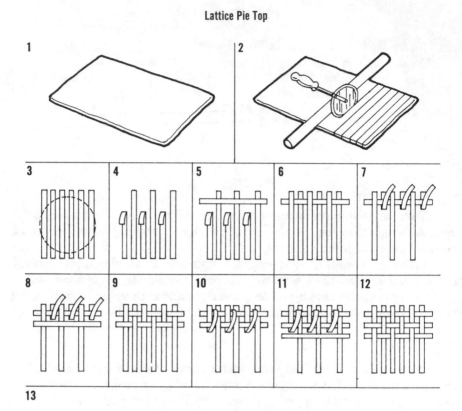

PIE FILLINGS

There are five main types of pie fillings.
1. Fruit pie. The most popular fruit pies are apple, pineapple, apricot, peach, and prune. The fruit used may be fresh, frozen, canned, dried, or prepared pie filling.
2. Cream pie.
3. Chiffon pie.
4. Soft pie.
5. Specialty pies.

Fruit Pie Filling Preparation

Among the many methods used in filling pies today, the following are the most generally accepted.

Cooked Juice Method: Drain the juice from fruit and bring to a boil. Thicken with the proper amount of dissolved cornstarch. Bring back to a boil to clarify and ensure the proper setting of the starch. Add granulated sugar, salt, spices, butter, or other flavoring agents and stir until dissolved. Pour over the drained fruit and stir carefully so as not to crush or mash the fruit. When the filling is cold it is ready for the pies. This method is generally used for cherry, apple, blueberry, apricot, and peach pies.

Cooked Fruit and Juice Method: Bring juice and fruit to a boil. Add the amount of dissolved cornstarch needed to bring the juice and fruit to the proper consistency. After the cornstarch is added, always bring the filling back to a boil so that it will clarify. Add the desired amount of sugar and stir until thoroughly dissolved. Care should be taken when cooking the fruit to stir occasionally to prevent scorching. When the filling is cold, it is ready for the pies. This method is generally used for raisin, pineapple, and apple pies if the latter are unusually hard.

Home-made Method: Mix the fruit with spices, flour, and sugar. Fill the unbaked pie shells. Place a lump of butter or margarine on top of the filling. Cover the pie and bake as usual. This method is very simple. However, the flour in the filling has a tendency to remain uncooked and the consistency is not as easily controlled as in the preceding two methods.

Cream Pie Filling

Vanilla, chocolate, butterscotch, banana, and coconut are the most popular cream pies.

Care should be taken to acquire a good smooth cream with a delicate flavor. This cream filling is always placed into prebaked pie shells.

Cream Pie Method: Place the milk with part of the sugar in a round-bottomed pan and scald. Mix the egg yolks, balance of sugar, starch, and flour into a paste. Add part of milk to make mix into liquid form. When the first part is near the boiling point, add the egg mixture and continue to stir until the filling comes to a boil. Remove from heat. Add the necessary flavoring to this mixture and stir. Place in prebaked pie shells. After cooling, top with meringue or whipped cream.

Chiffon Pie Filling

Chiffon pies are mixed similarly to the cooked fruit and juice method under fruit filling or the cream pie method. Meringue is folded into this mixture. Both cream pies and fruit pies may be converted into chiffon pies.

Chiffon Pie Method: Place in a pan the fruit, sugar, flavoring, coloring, salt, and water or milk. Bring to a boil on top of the stove. Dissolve the starch in juice or water, mix with the first part and continue to boil. Remove from heat. Make meringue with egg whites and sugar. Fold the meringue into the above mixture *immediately* while it is still hot. Place the mixture into a pre-baked pie shell. Remember to fill the shell generously, pyramiding it into the shell with a spatula. Allow pie to cool and top with whipped cream.

Soft and Specialty Pies

Pumpkin, sweet potato, squash, custard, and pecan pies are known as "soft" pies. They require a deep pie plate with an additional fluted pie crust rim.

Soft pies are made with an unbaked crust and uncooked filling. The filling is "set" during the baking process as it contains eggs, which help in the coagulation.

Each one of the soft pies is made in accordance with a specific formula developed in the following pages.

Nesselrode, ice cream, and Boston cream pies are known as "specialty" pies. They are made by a combination of the foregoing methods and are developed from formulas in the following pages.

Thickening agents

Starches and flour are used as thickening agents in pie fillings. Starches are used more often since they do not have a tendency to discolor and become gummy.

The amount used depends upon the jelling quality of the starch, the amount of liquid in the filling, and the desired consistency of the finished pie. Approximately two to five ounces of cornstarch for each quart of liquid (juice plus water) are used in the preparation of different fillings.

Ordinary Pie Faults and Their Causes

Faults	Overmixed	Insufficient shortening	Too much shortening	Improperly mixed	Insufficient liquid	Too much liquid	Improper flour	Overworking of dough	Baking temperature too low	Baking temperature too high	No bottom oven heat	Excess acidity in filling	Hot filling used	Lack of opening on top crust	Improperly sealed crusts	Filling too thin	Wet pie plates	Boiling over of filling	Too much sugar	Insufficient sugar	Watery egg whites	Not beaten firm enough
Pie dough																						
Stiff	X	X			X																	
Crumbly	X	X	X	X	X		X															
Tough				X			X															
Baked crust																						
Shrinkage	X	X				X	X	X														
Solid crust		X				X	X															
Too light in color									X													
Tough	X	X				X	X	X														
Two-crust pies																						
Unbaked crust bottom				X					X		X	X	X				X					
Boiling of filling during baking												X	X	X	X	X						
Crust sticking to pans		X									X						X	X	X			
Crust soaked on bottom			X						X		X	X	X			X	X	X				
Meringue																						
Watery or weeping				X					X										X	X	X	X
Tough				X						X										X	X	

PIE CRUST (*for general use*)

Pastry flour	3 lb	
Shortening	2 lb	
Salt		1 oz
Cold water or milk (1 pint)	1 lb	
	6 lb	1 oz

Method: Rub shortening into flour to form nuggets the size of walnuts. Dissolve salt in liquid. Add and mix with flour and shortening.
Baking instructions: 400°-425°F.

GRAHAM CRACKER CRUST

Graham crackers, ground	1 lb	
Butter, melted		6 oz
Sugar		6 oz
	1 lb	12 oz

Method: Mix crumbs and sugar. Add melted butter. Rub with your hands until it has a wet sandy consistency. Pour crumb mixture into 9-inch pie plate. Set 8-inch pie plate on top of crumbs and press firmly to make an even layer of crumbs. Crust shell is now ready to fill and use as is, to freeze for ice cream pie or to bake in 375°F oven for 8 minutes to obtain a crisper crust and extra flavor. (Makes approximately four 9-inch pie crusts.)

APPLE PIE FILLING (*canned*)

Apples, 1 No. 10 can	6 lb	8 oz
Water (1 qt)	2 lb	
Sugar	1 lb	8 oz
Salt		½ oz
Cinnamon		¼ oz
Nutmeg		1/8 oz
Butter		1½ oz
Cornstarch		3 oz
	10 lb	5-3/8 oz

Method: Bring to a boil all ingredients except cornstarch and 8 oz water. Dissolve cornstarch in water and add to mixture. Bring the mixture to a boil and remove from heat.
Scaling instructions: Five 9-inch pies.
Baking instructions: 425°F.

Streusel topping: For apple-raisin filling, add 8 ounces of raisins.

APPLE PIE FILLING *(frozen)*

Apples (frozen)	10 lb	
Water (1¼ qt)	2 lb	8 oz
Sugar	1 lb	8 oz
Salt		½ oz
Cinnamon		1/8 oz
Nutmeg		1/8 oz
Water (½ pint)		8 oz
Cornstarch		5 oz
Lemon juice (2 lemons)		
Butter		3 oz
	15 lb	¾ oz

Method: Bring apples, water, sugar, and spices to a boil. Dissolve cornstarch in water and add. Cook to a boil and remove from heat. Add juice and butter and mix well.

Scaling instructions: Eight 9-inch pies.
Baking instructions: 425°F.

BASIC CREAM FILLING or PASTRY CREAM FILLING

Milk (1¾ pint)	1 lb	12 oz
Sugar		3 oz
Sugar		3 oz
Egg yolks		3 oz
Cake flour		1½ oz
Cornstarch		1 oz
Milk		4 oz
Butter		½ oz
Vanilla (to taste)		
	2 lb	12 oz

Method: Boil milk and sugar. Mix together sugar, yolks, flour, cornstarch, and milk, and add to hot milk and sugar, stirring continuously until mixture comes to a boil. Remove from heat. Stir butter and vanilla into mixture.

Scaling instructions: Two 9-inch pies.

Chocolate filling: Add 1½ oz of melted chocolate.

Banana cream filling: Slice into filling approximately 1 banana per pie.

Coconut cream filling: Add 2 oz of coconut per pie into mixture. Top with whipped cream.

RAISIN PIE FILLING

Raisins	3 lb	
Brown and granulated sugar	1 lb	
Water (2 qt)	4 lb	
Salt		¼ oz
Lemon (1 lemon)		
Cinnamon		1/8 oz
Water (½ pint)		8 oz
Cornstarch		1 oz
Butter		1 oz
	8 lb	10-3/8 oz

Method: Boil together raisins, sugar, water, salt, lemon, and cinnamon. Dissolve cornstarch in 8 oz water and add to mixture. Bring to a boil and remove from heat. Add butter.
Scaling instructions: Four 9-inch pies.
Baking instructions: 425°F.

CUSTARD PIE and COCONUT CUSTARD PIE FILLING

Milk (1 qt)	2 lb	
Sugar		6 oz
Vanilla (to taste)		
Nutmeg (to taste)		
Eggs		10 oz

Method: Beat all together.
Scaling instructions: Two 9-inch pies.
Baking instructions: Start at 450°F for 10 minutes and finish at 375°F.

Coconut custard pie: butter coconut slightly, place in pie shell, pour mixture into shell, and bake.

CHERRY PIE FILLING

Cherry juice (1 No. 10 can)		
Sugar	1 lb	
Salt		½ oz
Red color (2 drops)		
Cornstarch		4 oz
Water		4 oz
Cherries, drained (1 No. 10 can)		
Butter		1 oz

Sugar	1 lb	8 oz
Lemon juice (1 lemon)		
	3 lb	1½ oz

Method: Bring cherry juice, sugar, salt, and coloring to a boil. Dissolve cornstarch in water and add to mixture. Bring to a boil and remove from heat. Add remaining ingredients.

Scaling instructions: Five 9-inch pies.

Baking instructions: 425°F.

CHERRY PIE FILLING (*frozen*)

Cherry juice, drained from cherries	3 lb	
Sugar	1 lb	
Salt		¼ oz
Red color (3 drops)		
Water		8 oz
Cornstarch		5 oz
Sugar	1 lb	
Cherries, drained	7 lb	
Lemon juice (1 lemon)		
	12 lb	13¼ oz

Method: Bring cherry juice, sugar, salt, and coloring to a boil. Dissolve cornstarch in water and add. Bring to a boil and remove from heat. Add sugar, cherries, and lemon juice and mix in well.

Scaling instructions: Six 9-inch pies.

Baking instructions: 425°F.

APRICOT PIE FILLING (*frozen*)

Apricots (frozen)	10 lb	
Water (1 pint)	1 lb	
Salt		¼ oz
Sugar	1 lb	
Yellow color (2 drops)		
Water (½ pint)		8 oz
Cornstarch		5 oz
	12 lb	13¼ oz

Method: Boil together apricots, water, salt, sugar, and coloring. Dissolve cornstarch in water and add to other ingredients. Cook to a boil and remove from heat.

Scaling instructions: Six 9-inch pies.

Baking instructions: 425°F.

SWISS CHEESE PIE

Swiss cheese, grated	8 oz
Parmesan cheese, grated	8 oz
Egg yolks (4)	
Salt and pepper (to taste)	
Light cream (1 qt)	2 lb
Eggs (3)	6 oz
Onion, chopped fine (1 small)	
Bacon, crisp, chopped fine	8 oz
Parsley, chopped fine	

Method: Scald cream and mix cheeses, yolks, salt, pepper, and eggs into a custard. Sprinkle onion, bacon, and parsley on bottom of a prebaked pie shell. Pour custard mix over top.

Baking instructions: 350°-375°F for 10-15 minutes.

PINEAPPLE CHIFFON PIE FILLING

Pineapple, crushed	2 lb	
Sugar	1 lb	
Water (1 qt)	2 lb	
Salt		½ oz
Gelatin		¼ oz
Yellow color (3 drops)		
Cornstarch		5 oz
Water		5 oz
Egg whites		12 oz
Sugar		12 oz
	7 lb	2¾ oz

Method: Bring pineapple, sugar, water, salt, gelatin, and coloring to a boil. Dissolve cornstarch in water and add to mixture. Bring to a boil and remove from heat. Beat whites and sugar into a meringue and fold into mixture. Top with whipped cream and toasted coconut.

Scaling instructions: Four 9-inch pies.

PINEAPPLE PIE FILLING (No. 2)

Pineapple, crushed (1 No. 10 can)	6 lb	8 oz
Salt		¼ oz
Corn syrup		8 oz
Sugar	1 lb	8 oz
Yellow color (3 drops)		

Water (1½ pint)	1 lb	8 oz
Cornstarch		3 oz
Water (½ pint)		8 oz
	10 lb	11¼ oz

Method: Combine pineapple, salt, corn syrup, sugar, water, and coloring and bring to a boil. Dissolve cornstarch in water and add. Cook to a boil and remove from heat.

Scaling instructions: Five 9-inch pies.

Baking instructions: 425°F.

BLUEBERRY PIE FILLING (*frozen*)

Blueberry juice, drained from blueberries	1 lb	
Water (1 pint)	1 lb	
Sugar	1 lb	8 oz
Salt		¼ oz
Water (½ pint)		8 oz
Cornstarch		4 oz
Sugar	2 lb	
Blueberries, drained	9 lb	
Lemon juice (2 lemons)		
	15 lb	4¼ oz

Method: Bring blueberry juice, water, sugar, and salt to a boil. Dissolve cornstarch in water and add. Cook to a boil and remove from heat. Add sugar, blueberries, and lemon juice and mix well.

Scaling instructions: Eight 9-inch pies.

Baking instructions: 425°F.

PEACH PIE FILLING

Peach juice (1 No. 10 can)		
Water (1 qt)	2 lb	
Sugar	1 lb	
Yellow color (3 drops)		
Salt		¼ oz
Water (½ pint)		8 oz
Cornstarch		3 oz
Sugar	1 lb	
Peaches (drained from No. 10 can)	6 lb	8 oz
	11 lb	3¼ oz

Method: Bring juice, water, sugar, coloring, and salt to a boil. Dissolve corn-
        starch in water and add. Cook to a boil and remove from heat. Add
        sugar and peaches and mix well.
Scaling instructions: Five 9-inch pies.
Baking instructions: 425°F.

LEMON PIE FILLING

Water (1 qt)	2 lb	
Sugar		12 oz
Salt		½ oz
Butter		1 oz
Egg yolks		3 oz
Cornstarch		3 oz
Lemon juice		4 oz
	3 lb	7½ oz

Method: Bring to a boil water, sugar, salt, and butter. Beat yolks, cornstarch,
        and lemon juice together and add. Bring to a boil and remove from
        heat.
Scaling instructions: Two 9-inch pies.

LEMON CHIFFON PIE FILLING

Water (1½ pint)	1 lb	8 oz
Sugar	1 lb	
Salt		½ oz
Gelatin		¾ oz
Egg yolks		8 oz
Lemon juice		8 oz
Cornstarch		4 oz
Water (½ pint)		8 oz
Egg whites	1 lb	
Sugar		10 oz
	5 lb	15¼ oz

Method: Bring water, sugar, salt, and gelatin to a boil. Dissolve yolks, juice,
        cornstarch, and water together and mix until smooth; add to mix-
        ture. Stir until the mixture comes to a boil and then remove from
        heat. Beat egg whites and sugar into a meringue and fold into hot
        mixture.
Scaling instructions: Four 9-inch pies.

Orange chiffon pie: Use 7 oz orange juice and 1 oz lemon juice.

CHOCOLATE CHIFFON PIE

Water (1 qt)	2 lb	
Gelatin		½ oz
Sugar		8 oz
Chocolate, bittersweet		4 oz
Salt		¼ oz
Milk		6 oz
Cornstarch		4 oz
Cream, heavy		6 oz
Vanilla (to taste)		
Egg whites		12 oz
Sugar		8 oz
	5 lb	¾ oz

Method: Bring water, gelatin, sugar, chocolate, and salt to a boil. Dissolve
cornstarch in milk, add to chocolate mixture, and bring to a boil.
Remove from heat and add cream and vanilla. Beat whites and
sugar into a meringue and fold into mixture. Place mixture into pre
baked pie shells.
Yield: Four 9-inch pies.

STRAWBERRY CHIFFON PIE FILLING

Strawberries, frozen	2 lb	
Water (1 pint)	1 lb	
Salt		¼ oz
Sugar		8 oz
Red color (few drops)		
Lemon juice (1 lemon)		
Gelatin		¼ oz
Cornstarch		4 oz
Water (½ pint)		8 oz
Egg whites	1 lb	
Sugar		12 oz
	6 lb	½ oz

Method: Bring strawberries, water, salt, sugar, coloring, juice, and gelatin to a
boil. Dissolve cornstarch in water and add. Cook to a boil until thick
and remove from heat. Beat whites and sugar into a meringue and
fold into hot mixture.
Scaling instructions: Four 9-inch pies.

Fresh fruit pie: Use 2 lb of strawberries and 1 lb of sugar. Substitute
raspberries for strawberries for raspberry chiffon pie.

NESSELRODE PIE FILLING

Milk (1 qt)	2 lb	
Gelatin		1½ oz
Sugar		8 oz
Egg yolks (8 eggs)		6 oz
Heavy cream (1 qt)	2 lb	
Sugar		4 oz
Nesselrode mixture*		10 oz
	5 lb	13½ oz

Method: Heat milk and gelatin to a boil. Mix sugar and yolks and add. Scald but *do not boil.* Remove from heat and cool. Whip cream and sugar until stiff and fold into mixture. Before doing so, be sure mixture is cool and starting to set. Fold in nesselrode mixture. Place in four pre-baked shells. Top with whipped cream and shaved chocolate.

*Nesselrode mixture may be purchased or it may be prepared as follows: Soak together two ounces each of cherries, pineapple, and raisins, three ounces of chestnuts, and one ounce of rum.

SOUTHERN CHESS PIE

Brown sugar, light	1 lb	
Cake flour		2 oz
Salt		½ oz
Milk solids		4 oz
Shortening and butter		8 oz
Brown sugar, light	2 lbs	
Eggs		12 oz
Vanilla (to taste)		
Water, hot (1 qt)	2 lb	
	6 lb	10½ oz

Method: Cream together sugar, flour, salt, milk solids, shortening, and butter. Beat in remaining sugar, eggs, vanilla, and cream. Add hot water in 3 stages.
Baking instructions: 400°F for 10 minutes; then 350°F until done.
Yield: 3 pies or 80 tarts.

Pecan pie: add chopped pecans.

SOUTHERN PECAN PIE FILLING

Pastry flour		2 oz
Granulated sugar		2 oz
Light Karo syrup (1½ qt)	3 lb	
Eggs, whole	1 lb	
Vanilla (to taste)		
Salt		½ oz
Butter, melted		3 oz
Pecans		8 oz
	4 lb	15½ oz

Method: Mix flour, sugar, and syrup together. Whip together eggs, vanilla, salt, and butter and add. Place 4 oz of pecans in each pie shell and pour mixture over this.

Scaling instructions: Two 9-inch pies.

Baking instructions: 325°F.

PUMPKIN PIE FILLING

Brown and granulated sugar	3 lb	
Bread flour		8 oz
Salt		1 oz
Cinnamon		½ oz
Cloves		¼ oz
Ginger		1/8 oz
Pumpkin (1 No. 10 can)	6 lb	12 oz
Eggs	1 lb	4 oz
Skim milk (4 3/8 qt)	8 lb	12 oz
	20 lb	5-7/8 oz

Method: Sift sugar, flour, and spices together. Add pumpkin, then eggs. Add milk.

Scaling instructions: Eight 9-inch pies.

Baking instructions: Let stand at least 3 to 4 hours before pouring into pie shell. Bake at 450°F for the first 10 minutes; then reduce heat to 375°F.

Squash filling: Substitute No. 10 can of squash for pumpkin.

Sweet potato filling: Substitute No. 10 can of sweet potatoes for pumpkin.

MINCEMEAT PIE FILLING

Beef or venison	6 lb	
Suet	1 lb	
Apples, chopped	4 lb	
Brown sugar	1 lb	8 oz
Raisins, seedless	2 lb	8 oz
Currants	2 lb	8 oz
Brandy (½ pint)		8 oz
Allspice		½ oz
Cloves		½ oz
	18 lb	1 oz

Method: Boil meat and run through a grinder with suet. Add remaining ingredients and mix well. Add meat stock if more moisture is needed.

6

Puddings and Sauces

Puddings are popular, economical, and profitable desserts. As with other products, careful preparation is necessary to obtain the best results. All too often, puddings are carelessly prepared. The result is a mediocre product.

There are five basic types of puddings. The three most popular in commercial food operations are boiled puddings, baked puddings, and chilled puddings.

Steamed puddings are usually served during the cold season. They are generally heavy and are served with a hot sauce. They may be very attractive if care is taken with the final preparation.

Soufflé puddings are adaptable to à la carte service. They must be made just before serving to secure lightness and fluffiness; otherwise, they will become heavy and soggy. Soufflés are not a wise choice for cafeteria service.

BASIC VANILLA PUDDING

Milk (1 qt)	2 lb	
Sugar		4 oz
Egg yolks		2 oz
Sugar		4 oz
Cornstarch		1½ oz
Vanilla (to taste)		
Butter		½ oz
	2 lb	12 oz

Method: Mix sugar and milk, and scald. Mix together yolks, sugar, and cornstarch, and add part of the milk. Add rest of milk and boil, then remove from heat. Add vanilla and butter and mix well.

Yield: 10 servings.

Variations: Chocolate or other flavoring.

BREAD AND BUTTER PUDDING

Milk (1 qt)	2 lb	
Sugar		4 oz
Salt (to taste)		
Vanilla (to taste)		
Nutmeg (to taste)		
Eggs		2 oz
Bread slices (10 slices)		

Method: Scald milk. Beat together sugar, salt, vanilla, nutmeg, and eggs, and add to milk. Remove crust from bread, slice thin, brush with butter, and cut each slice in half. Place bread slices in a pudding dish, overlapping each slice. Sprinkle with a few raisins and pour custard mixture over slices. Serve hot with cream.

Baking instructions: Place dish on a pan containing water and bake at 400°F until firm.

BASIC BLANCMANGE

Milk (1 qt)	2 lb	
Sugar		8 oz
Gelatin		¾ oz
Cream, whipped	1 lb	
	3 lb	8¾ oz

Method: Scald milk, sugar, and gelatin. Put aside to cool and set. Fold in whipped cream and pour into individual molds (rinsed with cold water). Chill. Serve with crushed fruit or cream.

Chocolate blancmange: Add 4 ounces of chocolate.

Coconut blancmange: Add 8 ounces of toasted coconut.

Nut blancmange: Add 8 ounces of nut meats.

OLD ENGLISH PLUM PUDDING

Suet (ground)	2 lb	
Sultanas	1 lb	
Currants	1 lb	
Brown sugar		12 oz
Lemon peel		4 oz
Orange peel		4 oz
Citron		4 oz

Salt		1 oz
Nutmeg		¼ oz
Allspice		¼ oz
Ginger		¼ oz
Lemon juice (2 lemons)		
Rum (1 pint)		
Eggs		8 oz
Bread flour	1 lb	
Bread crumbs	1 lb	
	8 lb	1¾ oz

Method: Boil together for 2 hours suet, sultanas, currants, sugar, peels, citron, spices, and lemon juice. Store in a well-covered container for about 1 week. Add rum. Add eggs and mix. Add flour and bread crumbs and mix. Fill containers about 7/8 full. Steam for about 2 hours. Serve with a brandy sauce or hard sauce.

PLUM PUDDING

Butter	1 lb	
Brown sugar	1 lb	
Salt		1 oz
Nutmeg		¼ oz
Allspice		¼ oz
Ginger		¼ oz
Eggs	1 lb	
Molasses	1 lb	
Rum (½ pint)		8 oz
Brandy (½ pint)		8 oz
Bread flour	1 lb	
Raisins and sultanas	3 lb	
Currants	3 lb	
Citron	1 lb	
Orange peel	1 lb	
Lemon peel		8 oz
Bread crumbs	1 lb	
	15 lb	9¾ oz

Method: Cream together butter, sugar, salt, and spices. Add eggs and mix thoroughly. Beat in molasses, rum, and brandy. Mix in flour and fruit peels and stir until smooth. Add bread crumbs and mix to proper consistency. Fill containers approximately seven-eighths full and steam for about 2 hours. Serve with brandy sauce or hard sauce.

TAPIOCA

Milk (1 qt)	2 lb	
Minute tapioca		2½ oz
Salt (to taste)		
Egg yolks		2 oz
Sugar		2½ oz
Egg whites (3)		
Sugar		2½ oz
Vanilla (to taste)		
	2 lb	9½ oz

Method: Boil milk and cook tapioca until transparent. Remove from heat and add yolks and sugar. Whip together. Whip sugar, whites, and vanilla into a meringue and fold into mixture.

Yield: 10 servings.

CABINET PUDDING

Milk (1 qt)	2 lb	
Sugar		6 oz
Eggs		10 oz
Vanilla (to taste)		
Sponge cake, plain		8 oz
Raisins		4 oz
	3 lb	12 oz

Method: Combine milk, sugar, eggs, and vanilla and cook into a custard. Butter 12 custard cups and dredge with sugar. Cut sponge cake into ½-inch cubes. Place cake cubes in the cups and sprinkle with raisins. Pour the custard over this. Place the cups in a pan with water and bake until custard is firm. Turn out on a serving dish and serve with a hot vanilla sauce.

Baking instructions: 400°F.

Diplomat pudding: Substitute diced candied fruit for the raisins. Proceed as above.

BROWNIE PUDDING

Cake flour	1 lb	
Baking powder		1 oz
Salt		¼ oz
Sugar	1 lb	4 oz
Cocoa		2 oz
Shortening, melted		4 oz

Milk (1 pint)	1 lb	
Vanilla (to taste)		
Walnuts		8 oz
Brown sugar	1 lb	8 oz
Cocoa		4 oz
Water, hot (1½ qt)	3 lb	
	8 lb	15½ oz

Method: Sift dry ingredients together and work in shortening. Mix in milk, add walnuts and vanilla, and place this mixture in a 12 × 18-inch pudding pan. Pour hot water on top of mixture in pudding pan.
Baking instructions: 375°F.

INDIAN PUDDING

Milk (1½ qt)	3 lb	
Yellow corn meal		8 oz
Molasses		8 oz
Sugar		4 oz
Salt		¼ oz
Ginger		½ oz
	4 lb	4¾ oz

Method: Cook milk and corn meal in a double boiler about 20 minutes and remove from heat. Add remaining ingredients and place in a deep pudding pan. Serve with ice cream.
Baking instructions: Two hours at 375°F in water bath, stirring pudding occasionally.
Yield: 10 servings.

COCONUT PUDDING

Granulated sugar	1 lb	8 oz
Butter		12 oz
Salt		½ oz
Egg whites	1 lb	8 oz
Shredded coconut	1 lb	
Cake flour	1 lb	8 oz
Baking powder		¾ oz
	6 lb	5¼ oz

Method: Lightly cream sugar, butter, and salt. Add egg whites and cream. Add remaining ingredients and mix until smooth. Fill steam-type pudding pans ¾ full and place cover on top. Steam for 1½ hours. Serve with hot vanilla custard sauce.
Baking instructions: 375°F.

CUP CUSTARDS

Milk (1 qt)	2 lb	
Sugar		8 oz
Eggs (6)		10 oz
Vanilla (to taste)		

Method: Mix together sugar, eggs, and vanilla, and add to milk. Place in 10 custard cups. Place in pan with water and bake until firm.
Baking instructions: 400°F.

Caramel custard: Boil together 2 lb of granulated sugar and 1 lb of water to 328°F or until it becomes a dark amber color. Pour ¼ inch of this syrup into dry custard cups. Place above custard mixture into same cups and treat as with cup custards. When baked and cold, turn custard out into a deep dish and serve.

BASIC VANILLA BAVARIAN PUDDING

Milk (1 qt)	2 lb	
Gelatin		1½ oz
Sugar		4 oz
Vanilla (to taste)		
Heavy cream		8 oz
Egg whites		8 oz
Sugar		4 oz
	3 lb	9½ oz

Method: Dissolve gelatin in part of milk and bring rest of milk and sugar to a boil. Remove from heat and add dissolved gelatin. Add vanilla after mixture cools. Whip cream and fold in. Whip whites and sugar into a meringue and fold in. Place in custard cups or pudding dishes and put into refrigerator to set. When set, unmold into cold serving dishes and serve with a sauce.

Variations: Chocolate, walnut, coffee, and strawberry.

BASIC VANILLA SOUFFLÉ

Bread flour	3 oz
Butter	3 oz
Milk	8 oz
Egg yolks	6 oz
Egg whites	8 oz
Sugar	6 oz
Vanilla (to taste)	
Salt (to taste)	

Method: Put together flour and butter into a paste. Bring milk to a boil and add to flour paste. Cook. Beat in egg yolks as for a cream puff mixture. Whip egg whites, sugar, salt, and vanilla into a soft-peak meringue and fold into above. Butter soufflé cups or soufflé dish and dredge with granulated sugar. Fill to top with mixture and bake until done. Serve with a vanilla-custard sauce.

Baking instructions: 400°F with water on bottom of pan.

Chocolate soufflé: Add melted chocolate with egg yolks and proceed as for vanilla. Serve with vanilla sauce.

Cheese soufflé: Add grated cheese with egg yolks and omit sugar from meringue. Dredge soufflé cups or dish with grated cheese instead of sugar.

BAVARIAN CREAM

Milk (1 qt)	2 lb	
Egg yolks (6)		4 oz
Sugar		8 oz
Gelatin, plain		½ oz
Heavy cream (1 pint)	1 lb	

Method: Heat milk. Beat together yolks, sugar, and gelatin, and add to milk, but *do not boil.* Whip cream and fold into mixture after it has cooled and started to thicken. Place into a mold or cup and allow to set until firm. Unmold and serve with a sauce.

Variations: Coffee, chocolate, walnut, or maple.

BLUEBERRY PUDDING

Sugar	1 lb	8 oz
Butter		12 oz
Salt		½ oz
Egg whites	1 lb	
Milk		12 oz
Cake flour	1 lb	8 oz
Baking powder		¾ oz
Cinnamon (to taste)		
Blueberries, fresh	1 lb	8 oz
	7 lb	1¼ oz

Method: Cream sugar, butter, and salt together lightly. Add whites and cream. Add milk. Sift together flour, baking powder, and cinnamon, and add and mix until smooth. Fold blueberries into this mixture. Fill steam-type pudding pans ¾ full and place cover on top. Steam for 1½ hours and serve with hard sauce or lemon sauce.

RICE CUSTARD PUDDING

Milk (1 qt)	2 lb
Rice	4 oz
Salt (to taste)	
Sugar	4 oz
Egg yolks (2)	1½ oz
Vanilla (to taste)	
Heavy cream	5 oz

Method: Boil milk, add rice and salt, and simmer until rice is tender. Mix together sugar, yolks, and vanilla, and add. Cook until thick, remove from heat, and cool. Add cream after it sets.
Yield: 10 servings.

FARINA PUDDING

Milk (2 qt)	4 lb	
Farina		6 oz
Egg yolks (4)		4 oz
Sugar		6 oz
Cream		8 oz
	5 lb	8 oz

Method: Boil milk in a double boiler. Add farina and cook to a mush. Remove from heat. Beat together remaining ingredients and add. Pour into pudding pans or dishes and bake in a water bath. Serve hot with cream.
Yield: 15 portions.
Baking instructions: 400°F.

SAUCES FOR PUDDINGS AND ICE CREAMS

There are three basic sauces from which a great many varieties may be made by the addition of various ingredients.

Cream sauce is the most popular. It is made from milk, sugar, eggs or egg yolks, and water, cooked to a very soft custard, flavored, and served either hot or cold.

Fruit sauce is made from fruit or fruit juice boiled with water and flavored. Lemon juice is then added and the whole is reduced or thickened with a small amount of starch. Then it is cooked until it becomes a thin, jellylike sauce.

Hard sauce consists of powdered sugar and butter, creamed lightly, and sometimes thinned down with cream or egg and flavored. Hard sauce is always served cold on hot puddings or dumplings.

CHOCOLATE SAUCE

Sugar	3 lb
Water (1½ qt)	3 lb
Corn syrup	1 lb
Bittersweet chocolate, chopped fine	2 lb
Sweet chocolate, chopped fine	2 lb
Heavy cream (1 qt)	2 lb
	13 lb

Method: Combine all ingredients except cream. Bring to a boil and stir. Boil heavy cream and stir in.

BUTTERSCOTCH SAUCE

Brown sugar	2 lb	
Water	1 lb	
Corn syrup		8 oz
Butter		8 oz
Heavy cream	2 lb	
	6 lb	

Method: Combine sugar, corn syrup, and water; bring to a boil until temperature reaches 320°F. Add butter. Add cream and place on fire for a few minutes. Use for ice cream sundaes.

LEMON CUSTARD SAUCE

Water (2 qt)	4 lb	
Sugar		8 oz
Egg yolks		8 oz
Cornstarch		1 oz
Coloring (few drops)		
Sugar		8 oz
Lemon juice		8 oz
Lemon rind (4 lemons)		
	6 lb	1 oz

Method: Bring water and sugar to a boil. Beat together yolks, cornstarch, coloring, and sugar. Add to water and thicken. Boil for 1 minute and remove from heat. Add lemon juice and rind and mix.

Orange sauce: Substitute oranges for lemons.

VANILLA CUSTARD SAUCE

Light cream (1 qt)	2 lb	
Egg yolks		6 oz
Sugar		8 oz
Vanilla (to taste)		
	2 lb	14 oz

Method: Bring cream to a boil. Mix yolks, sugar, and vanilla together and add. Cook until thick, but do not allow to come to a boil.

APRICOT SAUCE

Apricots (1 No. 10 can)	6 lb	12 oz
Water (2 qt)	4 lb	
Sugar	4 lb	
Lemon juice (2 lemons)		
Cornstarch		2 oz
Water (1 pint)	1 lb	
	15 lb	14 oz

Method: Press apricots and water through a fine sieve. Add sugar and lemon juice and bring to a boil. Dissolve cornstarch in water and add. Allow to boil 1 minute and remove from heat. Strain and cool. Sauce may be served hot or cold.

Peach sauce: Substitute peaches for apricots.

RASPBERRY SAUCE

Raspberries, fresh (2 qt)	1 lb	8 oz
Sugar	2 lb	
Lemon juice (2 lemons)		
Water (1 pint)	1 lb	
Coloring (few drops)		
Cornstarch		2 oz
Water		8 oz
	5 lb	2 oz

Method: Boil together raspberries, sugar, juice, water and coloring. Dissolve cornstarch in water and add. Boil for about 1 minute. Remove from heat and strain.

Strawberry sauce: Substitute strawberries for raspberries.

MELBA SAUCE

Raspberries, fresh	1 lb	
Currant jelly		8 oz
Sugar		8 oz
Water		2 oz
Cornstarch		1 oz
	2 lb	3 oz

Method: Boil raspberries, jelly, and sugar together. Dissolve cornstarch in water and add. Bring to a boil.

HARD SAUCE

Powdered sugar	2 lb
Butter	1 lb
	3 lb

Method: Cream lightly. Eggs or cream may be used to bring to the desired consistency.

Variations: Mocha, chocolate, or brandy may be added.

7

Icings

Attractive icings have three main functions: they form a protective coating around the cake, improving the keeping quality by trapping the moisture; they improve the taste; and they enhance eye appeal and make the cake a more attractive item for sale.

Proper combinations of flavoring are imperative. Only the best flavorings should be used. There is no economy in using cheap flavorings as they destroy the taste and quality of the entire product. Fresh fruit should be used for fruit icings when it is obtainable.

Care should be taken not to use food colors too lavishly as this will result in dark icings, which are not attractive. Delicate pastel colorings enhance eye appeal, but too much color cheapens the product. Color combinations should be studied carefully and tested for delicacy. It is better to err with too little color than to add too much.

BASIC ICINGS

There are seven basic icings: fondant, butter cream, fudge, flat, boiled, marshmallow, and royal.

Fondant is a syrup of glucose, sugar, and water, cooked to a temperature of 240°F. It is then cooled to approximately 110°F and worked quickly until it is creamy, white, and smooth.

Fondant is a difficult icing to make. When it is used in quantity, it has become customary to purchase a uniform fondant icing from a baker's supply house. When this is done, the prepared fondant should be stored in containers, covered with a damp cloth or with a small amount of water, to prevent it from drying out.

When fondant icing is to be used, the desired quantity should be taken out and heated over a warm bath to 98° to 100°F, stirring constantly. This thins the icing and causes it to flow freely. If it is still too heavy, a simple

Cake Decorating

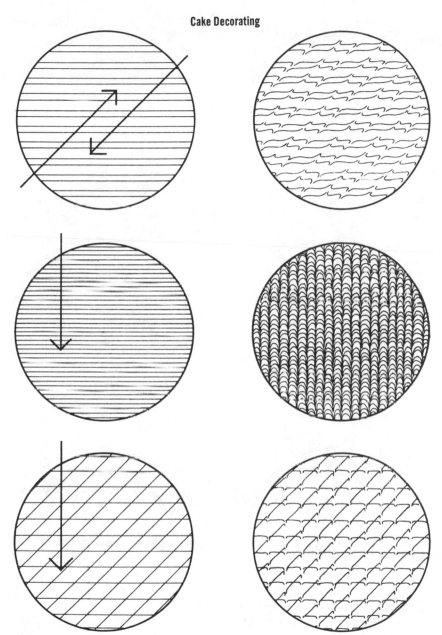

After icing has been put on the cake, a gentle action of a knife drawn in the directions indicated will give pleasing effects.

Cake Decorating

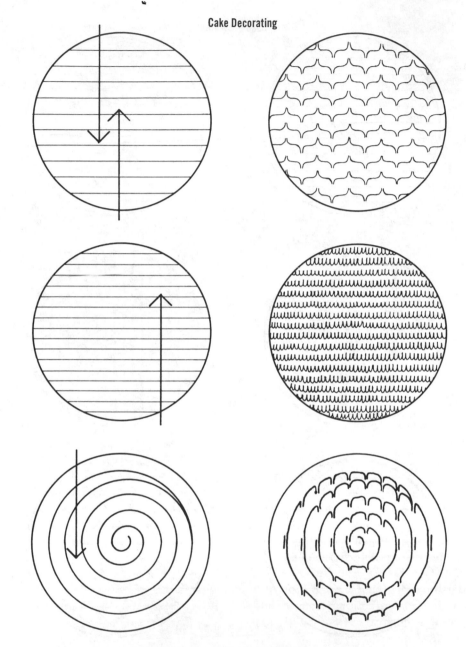

After icing has been put on the cake, a gentle action of a knife drawn in
the directions indicated will give pleasing effects.

syrup may be used to thin it more. Flavoring or coloring may be added as desired. Fondant icing should not be heated above 100°F or it will lose its glossiness and create a dull finish.

Fondant is used primarily for pouring and dipping. It may be used as a base for other icings such as butter cream by creaming the butter or shortening with the fondant. This creates fluffier icings.

Butter cream is made by creaming together sugar, butter or shortening, and eggs. The last are added to give the icing the desired consistency. The amount of creaming depends upon the lightness required in the finished product. Buttercream may be colored and flavored as desired. When not in use, this icing should be stored in a cool place with wax paper covering.

Butter cream is generally used for layer cakes and decorated cakes.

Fudge Icing. For fudge icing, the sugar is cooked into a syrup in order to obtain the smoothness required. When this hot syrup is added to the balance of the ingredients in the formula, it creates a rather heavy body. Before the icing is applied to the cake it should be heated slightly in a water bath. When it is not in use it should be stored and covered to prevent spoilage and drying.

Fudge icing is generally used on cupcakes and layer cakes.

Flat Icing or Plain Water Icing is a simple icing, whose basic ingredients—water, icing sugar, corn syrup, and flavoring—are mixed well together. Before applying this icing to coffee cake, Danish pastry, and the like, heat it to 100°F and apply by hand or pastry brush. Flat icing is usually white and flavored with vanilla or lemon. Coloring may be used, but very sparingly, if at all. It must be kept covered when not in use.

Boiled Icing is made by cooking a syrup of sugar, water, and glucose, which is then added to beaten egg whites while hot. A heavy or thin icing depends upon the heaviness or thinness of the syrup. Boiled icing may be flavored with vanilla and colored lightly. It should be applied generously and left in peaks on the cake. It breaks down if stored overnight and should be made only in the desired amounts as needed.

Marshmallow Icing is a variation of boiled icing, but it has a stabilizer—usually gelatin and confectioner's sugar—added to it. It is applied in the same manner as boiled icing.

Royal or Decorating Icing is also a fairly simple icing to make. Icing sugar, egg whites, and an acid agent are beaten together into a smooth consistency. Royal icing is used primarily for decorating and for flower making. It is also often used to make cake "dummies," but seldom used on stable cakes as it tends to become hard and brittle. It may be colored as desired and should be covered with a damp cloth when not in use.

FLAT ICING

Confectioner's sugar	5 lb	
Corn syrup		8 oz
Egg whites		4 oz
Water, hot		12 oz (variable)
	6 lb	8 oz

Method: Mix ingredients until smooth. Heat icing as needed and apply only to precooled products. Use it for coffee cake, Danish pastry, etc.

PLAIN ICING

Confectioner's sugar	5 lb	
Water		8 oz
Egg whites		1 oz
Corn syrup		4 oz
	5 lb	13 oz

Method: Mix ingredients together until smooth. This icing is an excellent substitute for fondant icing. It must be heated to 98°F and flavored the same as for fondant.

MARSHMALLOW ICING

Water, cold (1 qt)	2 lb	
Gelatin (plain granular)		3 oz
Corn syrup	1 lb	
Confectioner's sugar	6 lb	8 oz
Salt		½ oz
Vanilla (to taste)		
Egg whites		8 oz
	10 lb	3½ oz

Method: Soak gelatin in water, and heat until dissolved. Add sugar, syrup, salt, and vanilla, and mix. Add whites and beat to a proper consistency. Use this icing directly after mixing. For a more tender icing, add 3 ounces of shortening for each pound of icing.

ROYAL OR DECORATING ICING

Confectioner's sugar	2 lb	
Egg whites		6 oz (variable)
Cream of tartar (¼ teaspoon)		

Method: Beat together until stiff. Use for decorating dummies, making
 flowers, lattice work, etc. Keep covered with a damp towel when
 not in use.

FONDANT ICING

Granulated sugar	10 lb
Water (1 qt)	2 lb
Corn syrup	1 lb
	13 lb

Method: Boil ingredients to approximately 240°F. Pour hot syrup on wet marble slab. Sprinkle water over hot syrup to prevent it from crystalliz-
 ing. Allow it to cool to about 110°F. Work with a spatula from the
 sides to the center until the syrup becomes stiff and white in color.
 Remove from marble. Place in a storage container and cover tightly
 with a damp cloth. Use as needed.

WHITE FUDGE ICING

Milk (1 pint)	1 lb (variable)	
Shortening, emulsified		8 oz
Butter		8 oz
Salt		¼ oz
Confectioner's sugar	7 lb	
Vanilla (to taste)		
	9 lb	¼ oz

Method: Heat milk, shortening, butter, and salt to 160°F. Add sugar and
 vanilla and mix until smooth. Icing will be easier to apply while it
 is still warm.

BOILED ICING

Egg whites	2 lb	
Salt		1 oz
Granulated sugar	4 lb	
Glucose		8 oz
Water (1 pint)	1 lb	
	7 lb	9 oz

Method: Beat whites and salt slowly to a wet peak. Boil sugar, glucose, and
 water to 240°F and add slowly to egg whites. Beat to the proper
 consistency. Make only enough for immediate use.

BUTTER CREAM ICING

Confectioner's sugar	10 lb	
Shortening, emulsified	2 lb	8 oz
Butter	2 lb	8 oz
Salt		½ oz
Flavoring (to taste)		
Egg whites	1 lb	
Lemon juice		1 oz
	16 lb	1½ oz

Method: Cream together lightly sugar, shortening, butter, salt, and flavoring. Add egg whites and lemon juice and cream to desired lightness.

FRENCH BUTTER CREAM ICING

Eggs (4 whole)		8 oz
Egg yolks (8)		6 oz
Sugar	4 lb	
Water (1 pint)	1 lb	
Butter	3 lb	
Shortening, Hi-ratio	1 lb	
Vanilla (to taste)		
	9 lb	14 oz

Method: Whip eggs and yolks until light. Cook sugar and water to 238°F and beat into eggs until cool. Add butter and shortening and whip. Add vanilla.

MAKING AND USING THE PAPER CONE

Practically any design or pattern may be made with a paper cone. Cut wax, or preferably parchment, paper into a triangle-shaped piece. Then roll the paper into shape. Fill the cone with the desired icing, roll the top down, and snip off the bottom to the desired shape or size. Royal icing is by far the most economical to use for practice work.

The use of a paper cone requires practice. Too often the student starts practicing on a design that is too complicated. One should start with a series of straight lines until the right pressure and pull of the icing is acquired. Practice and practice only will give the right dexterity and perfection desired.

Many designs may be copied with the aid of a paper cone, such as birds, flowers, and latticework. One who can master this type of work can be of extra value to himself and to his trade.

Decorating Cones

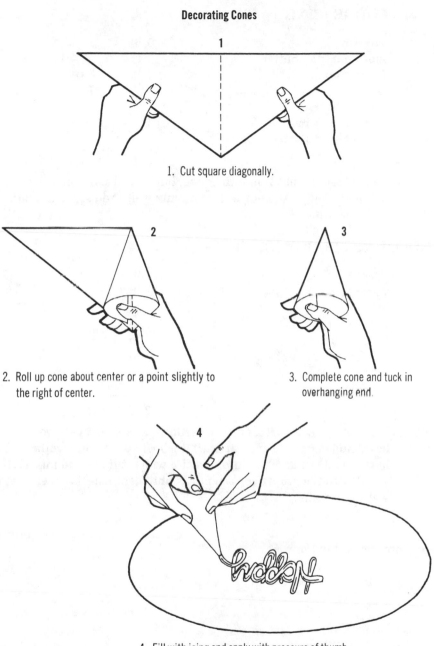

1. Cut square diagonally.

2. Roll up cone about center or a point slightly to the right of center.

3. Complete cone and tuck in overhanging end.

4. Fill with icing and apply with pressure of thumb, using other hand to steady the cone.

DEVIL FUDGE ICING

Cocoa	1 lb	
Shortening and butter	1 lb	
Corn syrup	1 lb	8 oz
Salt		1 oz
Vanilla (to taste)		
Water, hot (1 pint)	1 lb (variable)	
Confectioner's sugar	5 lb	
	9 lb	9 oz

Method: Cream together until smooth cocoa, butter and shortening, syrup, salt, and vanilla. Add hot water and mix well. Add sugar and mix until smooth.

CHOCOLATE FUDGE ICING

Granulated sugar	3 lb	
Water (1 pint)	1 lb	
Salt		¼ oz
Corn syrup	1 lb	
Bitter chocolate	1 lb	
Confectioner's sugar	1 lb	8 oz
Butter		4 oz
Vanilla (to taste)		
	7 lb	12¼ oz

Method: Boil sugar, water, salt, and corn syrup to 238°F and remove from heat. Add chocolate and stir until it is melted. Cream together sugar, butter, and vanilla. Pour into mixture while still hot and mix at slow speed until the proper consistency is obtained. Icing is easier to apply while still warm.

DECORATING BIRTHDAY CAKES

Prepare a cake circle 2 inches larger than the cake and a doily 2 inches larger than the cake circle. Put a little icing between the cake circle and doily. Make sure cake is level and free of crumbs. Place a little icing between the doily and the cake before icing. This will hold the cake in place.

Icing. Place cake in center of circle and doily. Start icing the side of the cake to ¼ inch thickness. After the side is done, place icing in the center of the cake and spread to cover the complete cake.

Decorating. First place writing on cake. Second, put on the border. Put the flowers and other decorations on last.

PIPING JELLY CAKE TRANSFERS

Piping jelly is used to transfer pictures onto the top of a cake as a decoration. In the accompanying example, a Viking ship is used. First a suitable picture is chosen and a sheet of tracing paper is placed over it. The figure is then traced with black or brown piping jelly outline. The outline is then filled in with appropriate colors of piping jelly. This design is then allowed to dry overnight.

The cake is then prepared and iced to receive the jelly transfer. The transfer is placed on the cake, jelly side to the icing, with the paper side up. It is recommended that the surface of the paper be wet, either with a brush or cotton dipped in water, and allowed to stand a minute or so to facilitate release of the paper from the jelly. Peel the paper off, and you have the completed transfer of the original picture to the top of a cake.

Good sources for cake illustrations are children's coloring books and magazines. Piping jelly is available in neutral or in various colors.

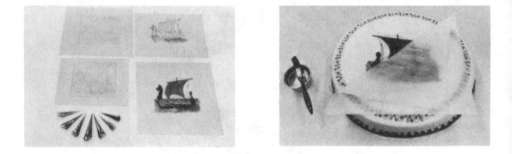

Piping jelly transfers.

8

Assorted Pastries and Desserts

The modern pastry chef and baker realize that they must have many variations in their desserts in order to attract new patrons. Although fancy pastries are usually referred to as "French pastries," many nations have contributed hundreds of popular variations to these popular desserts.

Some pastries and desserts are known in the trade as standard types. They may be greatly improved by developing variations and creating special names for them in the hotels and restaurants where they are prepared.

The finest quality ingredients obtainable must be used for these pastries. Patient craftsmanship is necessary for a fine finished product.

Originality and ingenuity, plus careful selection for variety, of pastries and desserts have created a famous reputation for many hotels and restaurants.

PUFF PASTE AND PUFF PASTE VARIATIONS

Puff paste is a rolled pastry from which a large variety of flaky, fine-tasting products are made. It is a rich dough to which additional butter is worked in. Great care must be taken in preparing and rolling the paste or the finished product will not be up to standard. The following rules should be observed when preparing puff paste:

1. Scale and prepare the dough strictly according to the formula.
2. When the butter or puff paste shortening is rolled into the dough, the butter and dough must be of the same consistency. Poor dough will result if either is stiffer than the other.
3. In warm climates or workshops, the dough should be refrigerated after it has been rolled.
4. Care must be taken that every particle of the puff paste or butter is evenly distributed through the dough. All ends and corners should be folded squarely.
5. Before folding over the dough, a minimum wait of 20 to 30 minutes should be allowed and all excess flour should be brushed off.
6. If paste is left over from the preceding day, it will require additional

rolling before being cut into units. Otherwise, the dough will not develop properly.

7. After the dough is cut into units, it should stand 20 to 30 minutes before baking. This prevents excessive shrinking.
8. Puff paste should be baked until it is dry and crisp.

No other baked product is quite like puff paste. It contains no sugar or leavening agent yet it rises to eight times its original size. This is due to the process of rolling alternate layers (which run well over 1,000) of fat and dough. A unit one-fourth of an inch high will sometimes rise more than two inches, with hundreds of fine, tender, crisp flakes.

Some bakers believe that the addition of cream of tartar helps the dough to rise. The author does not agree with this. It may make the dough shorter and easier to roll, but properly made puff paste will rise without cream of tartar to help it.

PUFF PASTE DOUGH

Bread flour	5 lb	
Salt		1 oz
Butter		8 oz
Eggs		8 oz
Water, cold (1 1/8 qt)	2 lb	4 oz
Butter for puff paste	5 lb	
	13 lb	5 oz

Method: Make flour, salt, butter, eggs, and water into a dough. Remove from mixer, round into a ball, and allow to stand for 15 to 20 minutes.
Roll butter into dough. Directions for this process follow.
Baking instructions: 350°-375°F.

Variations: Patty shells, vol-au-vent, cream horns, cheese sticks, cream slices, turnovers, napoleons, butterfly, etc.

ROLLING IN AND FOLDING PUFF PASTE

There are several ways of rolling the shortening into the dough. The method illustrated on page 127 seems the most satisfactory.

(1) Roll the dough, following the direction of the four corners, leaving the center somewhat thicker. (2) Place the shortening in the center and lap over the four sides. Flatten with a rolling pin by gently pounding the dough. Roll out again about one-half inch thick and twice as long as it is wide. After brushing off all the excess flour, fold both ends toward the middle and then double again. (3) Allow the dough to stand in a cool place or in the refrigerator at least 20 to 30 minutes before repeating the rolling process. Give four of these turns; the last roll is a "three-way fold."

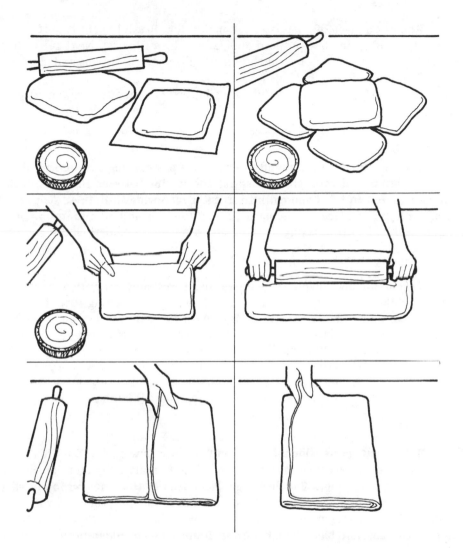

Rolling and folding puff paste.

Cream Slices

Roll out a piece of puff paste 1/8-inch thick. Brush the entire surface with water and sprinkle with sliced nuts (almonds or filberts). Next cut with a pastry wheel into 2-inch by 4-inch oblongs. Place on sheet pans and allow to stand 30 minutes before baking at 375°F.

After baking, split in two, fill with whipped cream, dust with powdered sugar, and serve.

Cheese Sticks

Give two turns to a 1-pound piece of puff paste, using two ounces of grated cheese mixed with salt and paprika for dusting between the folds. Roll out about 1/6 inch thick and cut into strips, 1 inch wide. Roll these strips into twisted sticks and place on wet sheet pans. Allow to stand 30 minutes before baking at 375°F. After baking, cut into strips 4 inches in length and serve.

Palm Leaves

Take a puff paste which is ready on five turns, and give it two more turns by rolling into fine granulated sugar. Then roll into a long strip, fold the sides to the middle so that the ends meet in the center, press well together with a rolling pin, and fold one side on top of the other. Now cut ¼-inch leaves from this strip with a sharp knife, place cut side down on clean pans, and bake at 375°F. When they are half baked, turn the strips over with a palette knife and finish baking to a nice golden brown color. For this it is best to use scraps of the puff paste and let stand for ½ hour before baking.

Butterfly

Take a puff paste which is ready on five turns, and give two more turns by rolling into fine granulated sugar; then roll out about 1/8-inch thick, and cut into long strips about 3 inches wide. Place four of the strips on top of each other, and press down in the center with a small rolling pin; then cut with a sharp knife into strips about 1/3-inch wide, twist the strips in the center, place on greased pans, and bake quickly at 375°F until a nice golden brown color is obtained. Remove from the pan as soon as they are taken from the oven, and place on a table or pan to cool.

Napoleons

Roll 1½ lb of puff-paste scraps very thin—the size of a baking pan. Place on a pan and allow to stand for a while. Prick the puff paste all over to prevent blistering while baking. Bake at 350°F.

After baking, cut into three strips and place together with a vanilla-flavored pastry cream. Frost the top with fondant of one or more flavors. When the fondant is dry, cut into bars about 4 inches long and 2 inches wide.

Patty Shells

Roll out a piece of dough about 1/8-inch thick. Cut out rounds using a 3-inch scalloped-edge cutter. Place these rounds on a clean wet baking pan.

Take another piece of dough and roll it ¼-inch thick. Be sure the thickness is uniform. Using the same cutter as before, cut a hole with a 2-inch cutter in the center of each round.

Wash the first rounds with water and then carefully place a second round on top of the first. Wash all with an egg wash and allow to stand at least 30 minutes before baking at 375°F. Greased paper placed over the top of the patty shells before they are placed in the oven will prevent the shells from toppling.

1-Napoleons. 2-Vol-au-Vent patty shell. 3-Cream slices. 4-Cream horns or lady locks. 5-Turnovers. 6-Cheese sticks.

Vol-au-Vent

Vol-au-Vent is a large patty shell, made in the same way as patty shells but somewhat thicker in proportion to the wider diameter.

Turnovers

Roll out a piece of dough about 1/8-inch thick and cut it into five squares. Wash the surface of the squares with water and fold cornerwise to form a triangle. Filling may be put into these turnovers before folding or they may be made without filling. Allow them to stand about 30 minutes before baking at 375°F.

If baked without filling, they may be split with a knife and filled with a variety of fruit fillings—apple, lemon, pineapple, etc.

Cream Horns (Lady Locks)

Roll the pastry into a strip about 15 inches wide and 48 inches long. When the rolling is completed, the pastry sheet should be no more than 1/8-inch thick.

Cut this sheet into strips about 1¼ inches wide. Wash the surface with water and roll each strip on a cream horn tin, starting the strip on the small end of the tin and following a diagonal direction. When the tin is covered, roll the horns in granulated sugar and then place in baking pans. Allow a short rest period to elapse before baking to reduce shrinkage.

Bake in a moderate oven until lightly browned. Remove the tins from the baked horns while they are still hot. When cool, fill the horns with marsh-mallow filling or whipped cream.

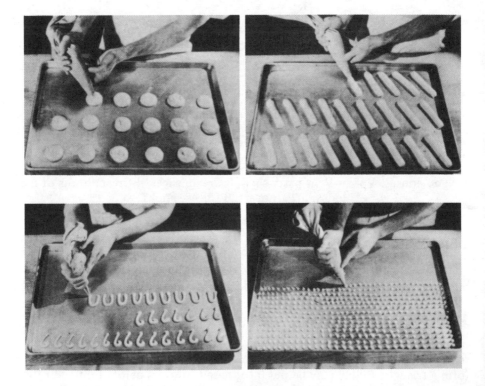

Top-Depositing cream puff shells and eclair shells. Bottom-Shaping basket handles and swan's necks from eclair paste, and making croutons with eclair paste.

Top-Turban, Croque-en-bouche, and Gâteau St. Honoré. Center-Whip cream eclair, Cream puff, Swan cream puff, Polka, and Beignet soufflé. Front row-Chocolate eclair, Chocolate whip cream eclair, Basket cream puff, Butterfly cream puff, Profiterole au chocolat, and French cruller.

CREAM PUFF AND ECLAIR PASTE

Water or milk (1 qt)	2 lb	
Shortening or butter	1 lb	
Bread flour	1 lb	8 oz
Eggs*	2 lb	8 oz

Method: Bring liquid and shortening to a rolling boil. Combine with flour and cook until the mixture is smooth and rolls free from the sides of the pot. Add eggs slowly until a medium-stiff paste is obtained.

Baking instructions: 400°F.

Variations: Cream puffs, eclairs, French crullers, and profiteroles.

SAINT HONORÉ

Saint Honoré consists of four parts: (1) short paste such as pie crust, (2) eclair paste or pâté à chou, (3) miniature puffs or small balls of eclair paste, and (4) pastry cream filling.

Roll out pie crust to an 8-inch diameter and 1/8-inch thick. Put small holes in crust to prevent blistering. Egg wash the edge of the crust. Pipe eclair paste on top of the edges of the pie crust, using a pastry bag with a plain round tube. Bake in oven at 400°F until done. When crust is cold, cut a ½-inch slice from the top of the shell. Fill edge with cream filling and put the top back on. Fill eight miniature puffs with cream filling from the bottom.

Cook 1/3 weight water to 2/3 weight of sugar at 325°F to make caramel sugar. Dip bottom of puffs in caramel sugar and arrange on the edge of the pie with the sticky side down.

For the center filling, use a basic cream filling and fold whipped egg whites into it. Fill center of shell with this mixture and garnish with a red cherry in the center and cherry halves between each miniature puff. Dust puffs with powdered sugar. Chill in refrigerator before serving. Serves 8.

APPLE STRUDEL

Bread flour, all-purpose	5 oz
Pastry flour, all-purpose	3 oz
Salt	1/8 oz
Egg (1 whole)	2 oz
Shortening	¼ oz
Water	4 oz
	14-3/8 oz

*The number of eggs varies. It is important that this mixture be of the right consistency or the product will be below par. Too few eggs will give a small product; too many will cause the product to spread.

Method: Mix ingredients into a smooth dough. Shape into a ball and brush with vegetable oil. Let dough relax for ½ hour. Spread dough on a 36 × 36-inch cloth and stretch thin and transparent (like tissue paper). This dough will make a 30-inch square. Brush entire surface with butter; egg wash bottom.

FILLING

Apples, chopped	2 lb	
Bread crumbs		4 oz
Brown sugar		2 oz
Granulated sugar		2 oz
Raisins		2 oz
Walnuts or almonds		2 oz
Cinnamon		1/8 oz
Lemon juice (½ lemon)		
Salt (to taste)		
	2 lb	12-1/8 oz

Method: Spread filling, leaving two inches on each side and fold ends under. Roll like a jelly roll, cut in half, and place on paper-lined pan. Brush with butter. Bake at 400°F for 45 minutes. Serve with whipped cream.

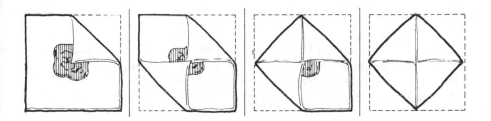

APPLE DUMPLINGS

Roll out pie dough approximately 1/8-inch thick and cut into 6-inch squares. Brush the squares with water.

Place apples that are about 3 inches in diameter, peeled and cored, on each square. Fill the center of the apples with a mixture of cinnamon sugar, fold as shown in the diagram, and bake at 400°F. Serve hot with lemon sauce or hard sauce.

Cause	Toughness	Excessive fat absorption	Lack of expansion	Excessive expansion	Excessive core	Knotty doughnuts	Fat absorption too low	Poor break (in frying)	"Balling up" of doughnuts	Tight, ringy doughnuts	Cracking on bottom	Cracking inside ring	Rough crust	Excessive spread
Machine speed too fast		X	X	X	X	X	X	X	X	X		X		
Dough too hot		X			X	X		X	X		X	X		
Dough too cold		X	X		X	X	X	X			X	X	X	
Doughnuts turned too soon after rising to fat surface				X			X	X		X				
Old shortening		X			X		X				X	X		
Insufficient cutter overlap								X	X			X		
Overmixing of dough	X		X		X	X	X	X		X	X			
Cutter size too small				X					X					
Undermixing of dough		X								X	X	X		
New shortening	X		X			X		X		X				
Dough too old			X					X				X		
Excessive cutter overlap			X			X		X						
Frying temp. too high	X				X	X	X	X	X	X		X		
Frying temp. too low		X			X					X	X		X	
Cutter in poor condition			X					X		X				
Dough too stiff			X					X	X		X	X	X	
Dough too soft	X	X			X	X		X		X			X	
Frying time excessive		X		X									X	

Doughnut Problems and Their Causes

RAISED DOUGHNUTS

Salt		1 oz
Sugar		6 oz
Shortening		6 oz
Flavoring (to taste)		
Eggs		8 oz
Water (1 qt)	2 lb	
Yeast		3 oz
Milk solids		4 oz
Bread flour	3 lb	8 oz
	7 lb	4 oz

Method: Mix into a straight dough. Ferment for 1 hour and 30 minutes. Always check: frying temperature frequently during frying, dough temperature, condition of fat, and condition of equipment.
Scaling instructions: 1 lb per dozen.
Frying instructions: Fry at 375°F.

CRULLER MIX

Sugar	1 lb	2 oz
Shortening		5 oz
Salt		¾ oz
Vanilla (to taste)		
Mace		¼ oz
Eggs (half yolks, half whole eggs)		8 oz
Milk (1 qt)	2 lb	
Cake flour	4 lb	
Baking powder		2 oz
	8 lb	2 oz

Method: Cream together sugar, shortening, salt, vanilla, and eggs. Add eggs and cream. Stir in milk. Sift flour and baking powder together, add to batter, and mix until smooth.
Scaling instructions: 1 lb per dozen.
Frying instructions: Fry at 370°F.

BABA AU RHUM

Milk (1 pint)	1 lb	
Yeast		2 oz
Bread flour		8 oz
Sugar		3 oz
Eggs	1 lb	8 oz
Salt		½ oz

Butter, melted		8 oz
Bread flour	1 lb	8 oz
Lemon rind, grated (1 lemon)		
	5 lb	5½ oz

Method: Make a sponge dough of flour, milk, and yeast. Add remaining ingredients and mix together into a smooth paste. Let this mixture rise for one hour, then place in forms. Let rise until double in size and bake. After baking, remove from forms and soak in rum syrup.* Garnish with whipped cream.

Baking instructions: 350°F.

*Rum syrup: Boil together 2 quarts of water, 2 pounds of sugar, the skin from 1 lemon, and 1 cinnamon stick. Add 4 ounces of rum.

SHORTCAKE BISCUITS

Cake flour	2 lb	
Salt		½ oz
Baking powder		2 oz
Powdered sugar		3 oz
Shortening or butter		12 oz
Eggs		4
Milk (1 pint)	1 lb	
	4 lb	5½ oz

Method: Sift together and blend dry ingredients. Rub in shortening. Beat eggs and milk together and mix. Split the cooked biscuits in half. Place on a dish with the fruit—strawberries or peaches—on top. Cover with the second half of the biscuit, top with whipped cream, and serve.

Scaling instructions: 3 dozen 2½-inch biscuits.

Baking instructions: 400°F.

CREPES SUZETTE

Cake flour		4 oz
Sugar		2 oz
Salt		1/8 oz
Lemon rind, grated slightly (1 lemon)		
Eggs		5 oz
Butter, melted		1 oz
Milk		8 oz
	1 lb	4-1/8 oz

Method: Melt butter. Sift sugar, salt, and flour together into a bowl. Beat together eggs and milk. Combine egg mixture with dry ingredients and mix until smooth. Add lemon rind and melted butter and mix thoroughly. Heat skillet until moderately hot. Pour in just enough batter to cover bottom of skillet. Tilt skillet or rotate it back and forth to spread batter thinly and evenly. Cook each crepe over medium heat until light brown on bottom side and firm to the touch on top side. Loosen edges with spatula, turn and brown other side. A slight coating of grease on the skillet may be needed after each crepe.

SAUCE FOR CREPES SUZETTE

Orange (1)
Lemon (1)
Sugar (4 lumps)
Butter (½ tablespoon)
Curaçao liqueur (1 tablespoon)
Grand Marnier (1 tablespoon)
Cognac (1 tablespoon)

Method: Rub sugar against the orange skin. Put them in the sauté pan, add a few drops of lemon juice and the juice of one orange and crush the sugar with a fork. Add the butter and stir well over the fire; then pour in the Curaçao and Grand Marnier. Bring mixture to a boil and remove from the fire. Fold the crepes and place them one by one in the sauce, pour the cognac over them and set on fire. Place the pan on the fire again, bring to a boil and serve very hot.

MERINGUES

There are many desserts and pies that can be made to look more attractive with the addition of a meringue topping. However, meringue is not always an easy topping to handle, as many bakers know. The methods described below may eliminate some of the difficulties.

In the first place, all utensils used in making a meringue must be scrupulously clean and free from grease. The egg whites must be clear and have a firm, jellylike consistency, containing no particles of egg yolks.

There are three types of meringue generally used:

COMMON MERINGUE

Egg whites	1 lb
Sugar	2 lb

Method: Beat the egg whites and gradually add the sugar. After all the sugar has been added, beat to the desired consistency.

ITALIAN MERINGUE

Egg whites	1 lb	
Sugar	2 lb	
Water		8 oz

Method: Beat the egg whites lightly. Cook the sugar and water to 244°F and add gradually to beaten egg whites in a slow, steady stream. Continue beating until the desired consistency is reached.

SWISS MERINGUE

Egg whites	1 lb
Sugar	2 lb

Method: Heat the sugar and egg whites in a bain marie or double boiler and whip until they are very warm. Then place in the machine and beat to the proper consistency.

MERINGUE SHELLS

Egg whites	1 lb	
Sugar	2 lb	
Salt		¼ oz
Vanilla (to taste)		

Making meringue shells.

Method: Make a meringue by adding sugar gradually while beating egg whites, salt, and vanilla. Beat until a stiff peak is formed. Make into nests or various shapes by pressing the meringue onto paper-lined pans with a pastry bag. Allow these to dry in a slow oven at 200°F. Serve with ice cream topped with melba sauce. Meringue sticks may be made by forcing the meringue through a pastry tube to form sticks which are sprinkled with nuts.

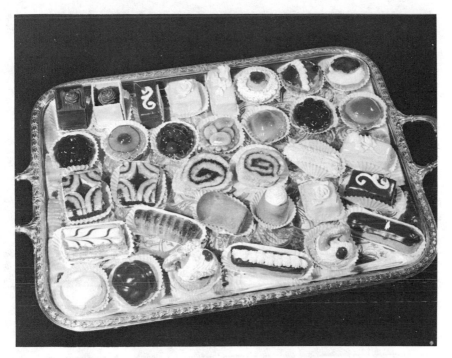

French Pastries

Top row-Chocolate boxes, Franchipan pastries, and Franchipan tartlets. Second row-Grape, pineapple, strawberry, banana, pear, cherry (Bing), and peach tartlets. Third row-Jelly roll fantasies and Franchipan pastries. Fourth row-Napoleon, Cream horn, Baba au rhum, and Franchipan pastries. Bottom row-Cream puffs, swan, eclair, basket, and eclair.

Chocolate Boxes

Heat sweet chocolate, spread it thinly on a papered pan, and let it cool. Cut it into 2-inch squares. Do the same with white chocolate. Split cake into two strips 2 inches wide, spread a layer of jelly or butter cream icing on one strip and sandwich the two layers together. The cake is then cut into 2-inch squares and the sides are masked with chocolate icing. The chocolate squares are then affixed to the sides of the cake squares. The boxes are then topped with butter cream or chocolate icing and garnished with a cherry or pistachio nut.

Franchipan Pastries

Various cuts of Franchipan cake are enrobed in fondant icing and then finished with the desired decoration.

Baba au Rhum

Unbaked dough is placed in a greased mold, proofed three times, and baked. The baked baba au rhum is then soaked in rum syrup and either topped or filled with whipped cream and garnished with a cherry.

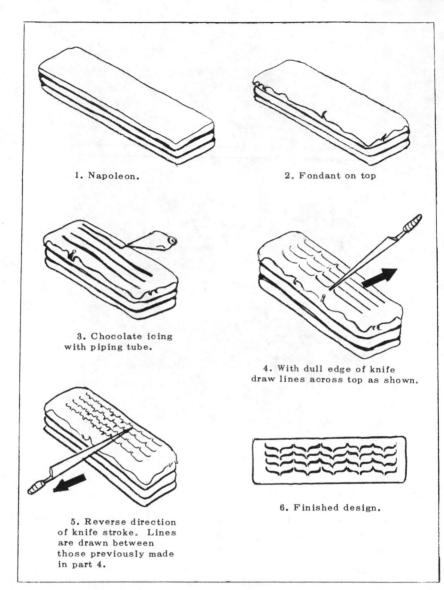

1. Napoleon.

2. Fondant on top

3. Chocolate icing
with piping tube.

4. With dull edge of knife
draw lines across top as shown.

5. Reverse direction
of knife stroke. Lines
are drawn between
those previously made
in part 4.

6. Finished design.

Napoleons

Take three strips of baked puff pastry, about 3½ inches wide, and spread pastry cream between the strips. Then, spread warm (about 98°) fondant icing over the top and decorate with lines of contrasting color. Finally, cut the finished product into slices.

Cream Horns

A strip of puff paste dough, 1¼ inches wide and 15 inches long, is wrapped around the cream horn stick and baked. The cream horn is then filled with pastry cream and topped with apricot glaze or powdered sugar.

Jelly Roll Fantasy

Cake is cut into 2½-inch squares and topped with butter cream icing. Jelly roll, filled with mocha, jelly, or lemon filling, is cut into slices and each slice cut into fourths. The pieces are rearranged to form a square. These squares are placed on the cake and the centers are filled with jelly, chocolate, or white fondant.

Cream Puff Baskets and Swans

Cream puff baskets and swans both use the bottom half of the cream puff shell as their base. The swan's neck and the basket's handle are separate pieces of shaped and baked pate a choux dough. The wings of the swan are made from halves of the baked shell's top. The finished basket or swan is filled with cream, garnished with a cherry, and sprinkled with powdered sugar. The cream puff shells themselves can be dipped in white or chocolate fondant icings and filled with pastry cream.

Eclairs

The eclair shells are baked and then either filled with pastry cream and dipped in chocolate or white fondant icing, or, split, dipped in chocolate or white fondant icing, and then filled with whipped cream.

Fruit Tartlets

Roll pie crust or short pastry about 1/8-inch thick and cut with a pastry cutter to 4¼-inch diameter. Press into tartlet pan and trim. Fill pastry ¾ full with rock salt, beans, or rice during baking of shell. After baking, fill shell ½ full with pastry cream and cover with sponge cake about ¼-inch thick and 1½ inches in diameter. Fruits such as peach, strawberries, pineapple, bing cherries (canned or fresh), pears, apricots, bananas, grapes, and blueberries can be used as topping. After the fruit has been put over the sponge cake, cover with hot apricot glaze.

Franchipan Tartlets

Put 2 ounces of Franchipan mixture into a tart pan and bake. Cut out, *not* to the bottom, a section from the center of the tart. Fill tart with pastry cream and sprinkle with powdered sugar. Cutout sections are topped with currant jelly and put on top of the tart.

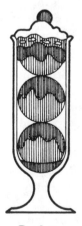

Parfait.

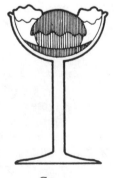

Coupe.

Parfaits

Parfaits are combinations of various colored and flavored ice creams, fruits, and sauces, topped with whipped cream. They should be served in tall, narrow glasses.

To make a parfait, place one spoon of crushed fruit in the parfait glass. Add a dipper of ice cream and cover with a spoonful of crushed fruit. Add another dipper of ice cream and cover again with crushed fruit. Add another dipper of ice cream and cover again with a spoonful of crushed fruit. Now cover with a spoonful of nuts in syrup and top with whipped cream. Decorate with a piece of fruit or nut.

Pour one or two tablespoons of sauce or syrup into a parfait glass. Place the ice cream in the glass and force it down into the syrup, which will work itself into a spiral around the inside of the glass. Top with whipped cream. Serve immediately or place in the freezer until serving time.

A few variations into which this popular dessert may be made are:

Melba: Vanilla ice cream with Melba sauce

Java: Coffee ice cream with chocolate sauce

Nesselrode: Vanilla ice cream with Nesselrode mixture

Rainbow: Vanilla, strawberry, and chocolate ice cream with strawberry
　　　　　sauce

Strawberry: Vanilla ice cream with strawberry sauce

Butterscotch: Vanilla ice cream with butterscotch sauce

Chocolate: Chocolate ice cream with chocolate sauce

Pineapple mint: Lemon sherbet with pineapple mint sauce

Coupe

In French, this word means "cup" or "goblet." It is also used to describe a dessert served in these dishes.

Coupes are made with ice cream, sherbet or ices, fruits and spirits, whipped cream, and sauces of various kinds. They are served in tall stemmed glasses or champagne glasses.

To make a coupe, place sauce or fruit in the glass. Add a dipper of ice cream, and cover with a sauce of fruit and spirits. Decorate with whipped cream.

Strawberry Coupe: Vanilla ice cream, strawberries, and whipped cream

Coupe St. Jacques: Maraschino, fresh fruit salad, raspberry and lemon
　　　　　　　　sherbet

Coupe Helen: Creme de Menthe, black Bing cherries, ice cream,
　　　　　　　whipped cream, and brandy

Pineapple Coupe: Ice cream, pineapple, whipped cream, and Kirsch

Coupe Melba: Vanilla ice cream, peaches, and Melba sauce

Coupe aux Marrons: Candied chestnuts, vanilla ice cream, and whipped
　　　　　　　　cream

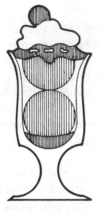

Sundae.

Banana Split.

SUNDAE

To make a sundae, place ½ oz of crushed, sliced, or whole fruit into a dish. Add two dippers of ice cream and surround the ice cream with 1 oz of crushed, sliced, or whole fruit. Add nuts and top with whipped cream and a piece of fruit.

BANANA SPLIT

To make a banana split, split a banana in half, lengthwise, with the peel on. Place one half on each side of the dish, flat side down, and remove the peel. Place three dippers of ice cream on the banana halves using vanilla in the center and other flavors on each side. Cover each dipper of ice cream with a different topping, ½ oz of each kind. Garnish the top and between the ice cream dippers with whipped cream. Sprinkle on nuts and add a piece of fruit.

MILK SHAKE

A milk shake is made by putting 6 oz of milk into a chilled cup and adding two dippers of ice cream and 1½ oz of syrup. Mix thoroughly and rapidly and pour into a serving glass.

ICE CREAM SODA

To make an ice cream soda, place 1½ oz of syrup into a 14 oz glass. Stir a spoonful of ice cream or 1½ oz of coffee cream into the syrup. Fill the glass three-quarters full with carbonated water and float two dippers of ice cream. Mix gently and add carbonated water to fill the glass. Top with whipped cream.

SPUMONI

Spumoni is an Italian molded ice cream with an outer layer of custard containing chopped almonds and an inner filling made with heavy cream, sugar, cherries, and candied orange peel.

To make spumoni, place chocolate ice cream into a mold to form the outer layer. Place strawberry ice cream on the chocolate ice cream to form the second layer. Repeat with vanilla ice cream. Fill the cavity with whipped cream or mousse with nut and fruit mixture. Freeze, unmold, and serve.

CASSATTA

To make cassatta, place pistachio ice cream into a melon-shaped mold to form the outer layer. Place strawberry ice cream into the mold to form the second layer, and repeat with chocolate ice cream. Fill the cavity with mousse or whipped cream with pistachio nuts. Freeze, unmold, and serve.

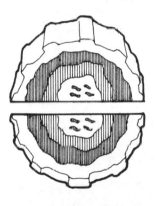

Cassatta.

ICE CREAM PIE

Place ice cream into a pre-baked pie shell (usually two different flavors are used), decorate the top with whipped cream, and serve with crushed strawberries. These pies may be made and then stored in a freezer until serving time.

SNOW BALL

Take a large scoop of ice cream and roll it in macaroon coconut. Put some chocolate sauce on a cold plate and place the ice cream ball in the center.

PEACH MELBA

Cut a round of sponge cake and place a scoop of ice cream in the center. Place a second round of sponge cake over the ice cream to form a sandwich. Place half a peach over this. Pour Melba sauce over all and garnish with whipped cream and sliced toasted almonds.

MERINGUE GLACÉ

Place a scoop of ice cream on a cold plate with a meringue kiss on each side. Pour Melba or strawberry sauce over the ice cream.

FROZEN ECLAIR

Fill an eclair shell with vanilla ice cream. Top this with chocolate or butterscotch sauce. Garnish with whipped cream and serve.

ICE CREAM PUFF

Stuff a cream puff shell with vanilla ice cream. Top this with chocolate or butterscotch sauce. Garnish with whipped cream and serve.

BAKED ALASKA

Cut a ½-inch thick sponge cake into an oval shape. Remove a portion of the center and place on a silver platter. Have on hand a meringue mixture. Fill the oval with vanilla ice cream, molding high as for a dome, and cover quickly with the meringue mixture. Decorate with this same mixture, forcing it through a pastry bag. Dust with sugar and bake at 450°F. Serve immediately.

PEAR HELEN

Place a piece of sponge cake on a serving dish. Top it with a scoop of ice cream. Place a pear half on the ice cream. Cover this with chocolate sauce. Garnish with whipped cream and serve.

CHARLOTTE À L'AMERICAINE

Apples, sliced	1 lb	
Butter		2 oz
Apricot sauce		4 oz
Pineapple, crushed		8 oz
Bananas, sliced		8 oz
Lemon rind (1 lemon)		
Kirsch		1 oz

Method: Heat butter and add apples and toss them over a good fire until tender. Add the apricot sauce and simmer a few more minutes, then fold in the pineapple, bananas, and lemon rind. Remove from fire. Add Kirsch and blend in. Serves 8.

Butter a charlotte mold, 4 inches high and 4½ inches in diameter. Cover the bottom with thin, round slices of white sandwich bread 1/8-inch thick (use stale bread, if possible). Arrange slices around the bottom and in the center so that they slightly overlap one another, carefully dipping them as needed in clarified butter. Then, cut some 1/8-inch thick slices of bread into 1-inch strips, having them the same height as the mold. Dip them in butter and place them upright and slightly overlapping one another around the inner side of the mold. Fill the mold with the fruit mixture and bake at 375°F for 1 hour or until the bread appears golden brown. Remove from oven and let cool. Pour over it a fruit sauce with Kirsch and serve some whipped cream separately.

Apple charlotte: Use 2 lb sliced apples in place of bananas and pineapple.

CHARLOTTE RUSSE

Line the sides of a charlotte mold with the required number of ladyfingers, previously trimmed. Then fill the mold with either Bavarian or whipped cream. Refrigerate until set. Unmold, decorate with whipped cream, and serve. These are quite often made as individual desserts in small paper cups or containers.

CHARLOTTE ROYAL

Line a charlotte mold with thin slices of jelly roll, and fill with either Bavarian or whipped cream. Unmold, decorate with whipped cream, and serve.

APPAREIL À BOMBÉ

Appareil à bombé is a base made for mousse or biscuits glacé mixture. It consists primarily of egg yolks, sugar, and water; it is prepared as follows: Cook 3 lb of sugar and 1 lb of water at 240°F, until a soft ball is formed. Place 24 egg yolks in a mixing machine and beat with a whip at medium speed. When sugar is cooked, pour it slowly on top of the eggs while they are beating in the machine, and beat until cold. When of a creamy consistency, remove from mixer and place in refrigerator until ready for use. This paste will keep for a week or longer. To each quart of cream that is whipped, fold in ½ lb of mixture. Add liqueur and fruit to suit the mixture; that is, Chocolate Mousse, Biscuit Tortoni, and the like.

Mousses

Mousses (chocolate, strawberry, coffee, mocha, etc.) are usually frozen in brick molds. They are cut into slices or served as larger pieces decorated with whipped cream, garnished with fruit, and served with a fruit sauce.

Biscuits Glacé

Biscuits glacé are desserts frozen in paper soufflé cups or cases, and then served in these same containers. The base for this dessert is the same as for the mousse mixture. The top of this dessert is generally decorated to harmonize with the flavor of the mixture.

BISCUIT TORTONI

Add 1 oz rum or brandy and 4 oz crushed macaroons to the mousse base. Fill the cups, using a star tube. Sprinkle with crushed macaroons, top with a maraschino cherry, and freeze. For bisquits glacé, coffee or mocha, follow the instructions above.

RICE IMPERATRICE

Water (1 pint)	1 lb	
Raspberry gelatin		4 oz
Rice, blanched	2 lb	
Milk (1 qt)	2 lb	
Salt		½ oz
Vanilla (to taste)		
Gelatin		1 oz
Sugar		8 oz
Heavy cream (1 qt)	2 lb	
Maraschino cherries, chopped		8 oz
	8 lb	5½ oz

Method: Dissolve gelatin in hot water. Place ½ inch on bottom of mold to be used and allow to set. Place rice, milk, salt, vanilla, gelatin, and sugar in a pot and cook and simmer for approximately 10 minutes. Allow to cool and set. Whip cream and fold in with mixture that has been set. Fold cherries into mixture, and place into molds or forms which have the gelatin set on bottom. Place in refrigerator until set. Unmold by setting forms in warm water and place on serving plates.

FRUIT CONDÉ

Milk (1 pint)	1 lb	
Rice, blanched	1 lb	
Salt		¼ oz
Sugar		4 oz
Gelatin		½ oz
Heavy cream (1 pint)	1 lb	
	3 lb	4¾ oz

Method: Place all ingredients except cream in a pot and simmer for approximately 10 minutes and allow to cool and set. Whip cream and fold in with mixture that has been set. Place this mixture in a large or small charlotte mold and refrigerate until mixture is set. When set, unmold on a dish and place assorted fruit on top of rice mixture. Brush top of fruit with a hot apricot sauce and serve.

PEACH CONDÉ

Prepare above rice mixture and place in a large, small, or individual charlotte mold and let stand and refrigerate until mixture is set. When set, unmold on a dish, place peach halves on top of rice, brush all over with hot apricot sauce, and serve.

Variations: Figs, strawberries, pears, and apples can be served in place of peaches.

BAVARIAN CREAMS AND CHARLOTTES

Milk (1 qt)	2 lb	
Egg yolks (6)		
Sugar		8 oz
Gelatin (plain)		½ oz
Heavy cream (1 pint)	1 lb	
	3 lb	8½ oz

Method: Heat milk. Heat together yolks, sugar, and gelatin and add to milk,
but do not boil. Whip cream and fold into mixture after it has cooled
and started to thicken. Place into a mold or cup and allow to set
until firm. Unmold and serve with sauce. Serves 12.

Variations: Coffee, chocolate, walnut, maple, or liqueur of any flavor. The
mixture is also suitable for preparing the various chilled Charlotte
desserts such as Charlotte Royale, Charlotte Russe, Strawberry
Charlotte, etc.

STRAWBERRY CHARLOTTE

Line the bottom of a plain charlotte mold with strawberry jelly; then
line the sides with ladyfingers and fill the center with a strawberry Bavarian
cream mixture. When set, unmold the charlotte on a cold dish and decorate
or garnish with whipped cream and strawberries. Variations can be made by
substituting peach, raspberry, apricot, or other fruits for strawberries.

Appendix

SUGAR COOKING

The ideal proportion of sugar to water is three parts sugar and one part water. These should be placed in a copper or stainless steel pot and stirred until the mass comes to a boil.

The sides of the pot may be brushed with water to clear them of any sugar crystals. Or the pot may be covered while the syrup is boiling, allowing the steam to wash down the sides. This is an important step in the early stages.

Continue to cook the syrup until it reaches the proper degree. Expert confectioners usually judge the degree of the syrup by dipping the index finger into cold water and then immediately dipping the same finger into the boiling syrup. This method is definitely not recommended for a novice because of the danger involved; a candy thermometer should be used. (When not in actual use, place the candy thermometer in a jar of warm water near the stove, eliminating the possibility of breakage, which often occurs when a cold thermometer is placed in hot syrup.)

The following chart indicates the boiling stages and the temperature readings for each stage. Since it only takes a few degrees to bring the syrup to another stage, temperature control is very important. It is also important to remember that temperatures in the chart below may vary because of differences in humidity and altitude.

Stages	Temperatures
Thread	230°-235°F
Soft ball	240°-245°F
Ball	250°-255°F
Hard ball	260°-265°F
Small crack	270°-275°F
Crack	275°-280°F
Hard crack	285°-315°F
Caramel	325°-350°F

157

The proportion of sugar and water varies as the cooking proceeds:

Temperature of Water and Sugar	Percent of Sugar Present	Percent of Water Present
212.7°F	10	90
213.8°F	30	70
215.6°F	50	50
223.7°F	70	30
225.2°F	75	25
238.8°F	85	15
243.8°F	87	13
249.5°F	89	11
252.7°F	90	10

Rock Sugar or Soufflé Sugar

Rock sugar is quite simple to make. It is appropriate for use for rock formations, bases for lighthouses made of sugar, etc. Rock sugar should be cooked in an extra large kettle, because the mixture rises and foams considerably. Have a wooden or cardboard box available to pour the mixture into when it is ready. If a wooden box is used, it should be lined with paper. A cake box 12 × 12 × 6 inches would be adequate for the amount of mixture in the following recipe:

Granulated sugar	3 lb	
Water (1 pint)	1 lb	
Corn syrup		5 oz
Egg whites (1)		

Method: Cook sugar and water to 280°F and remove from the heat. Whip together whites and syrup and add to heated mixture. Stir slowly with a wooden paddle. The mixture will bubble and foam and then appear to drop. Stir continuously until it rises for the second time. When the mixture starts to settle the second time, pour it into the box and it will rise. Allow it to set until firm. It will be porous and can be broken off into the desired sized pieces and stuck together with royal icing.

MARZIPAN

Marzipan is a candy which has a definite almond flavor. It is adaptable to many uses. It may be molded or hand carved into fruits, vegetables, animal figures, etc., or it may be used as a topping for cookies or cakes.

When using a mold with marzipan, it is best to dust the mold first with confectioner's sugar to prevent sticking. Remove the marzipan from the mold immediately and allow it to dry.

When colored appropriately with dry or liquid coloring, marzipan can be very attractive. There are a number of recipes for marzipan but the one below seems the most satisfactory.

Almond paste	1 lb
Confectioner's sugar	1 lb

Method: Rub together until fine. Either fondant icing, egg whites, or a simple syrup may be used to bring this mixture to a fine, firm consistency.

A picture frame made of marzipan.

Marzipan is a very versatile confection and an interesting medium for many confectionary creations. The following will give some ideas.

Begin with the proper tools: a plain or ribbed rolling pin; tweezers; bone or wooden sculpturing tools; and a blowtorch for the browning effect on some pieces. Other tools can be adapted as needed, such as a light bulb to give a curl to a flower petal.

The accompanying photo shows an unusual picture frame with a floral design, made entirely with marzipan of various colors. The borders are made separately from flat or ribbed marzipan (by using the plain or ribbed rolling pins) rolled about a cylinder. The cylindrical pieces are then decorated with the tweezers and sculpturing tools. The antique effect is accomplished with the blowtorch. The flowers and other designs are made by cutting and putting together small pieces of colored marzipan.

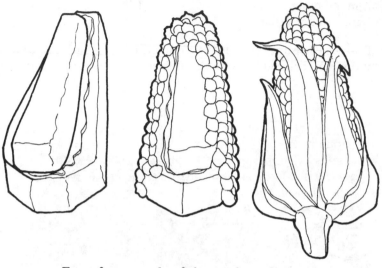

Ears of corn made of sheet cake and marzipan.

Specialty Cakes

Specialty cakes for Thanksgiving and other holidays can be made from marzipan by using the same basic principles illustrated here. To make an ear of corn, for example, cut a sheet cake into oblong pieces and cover them with dots of yellow butter cream icing to achieve the corn effect. The husk is made by rolling out marzipan, cutting it, and laying it in the cake in the proper position.

Another possibility for Thanksgiving is a turkey. This is made by cutting a sheet cake into the general shape of a roast turkey and masking it with butter cream icing. The entire cake is then covered with a thin neutral marzipan to give the turkey effect. Finally, the surface of the marzipan is covered with a caramel-colored glaze to give the finished cake the roasted effect that a turkey would have. As a finishing touch, cut fringes in a paper cylinder and put it on the legs of the "turkey."

Blown and Pulled Sugar

The sugar centerpieces shown in the accompanying figures are the work of Charles Camarano, a master pastry cook and candy maker. These attractive decorations are made of cooked sugar that has been pulled and blown. Mr. Camarano's techniques are described here.

Granulated sugar	5 lb	
Water (1 pint)	1 lb	
Cream of tartar		¼ oz
Salad oil (for use on marble slab)		
Assorted paste coloring		

Recipe and method of cooking sugar: Place 5 lb granulated cane sugar and 1 pint of water in a heavy pot, preferably copper, over medium heat. When sugar and water begin to boil add ¼ oz cream of tartar which has been melted in 1 tablespoon of water. Turn heat as high as possible so that the sugar cooks fast. Wash the sides of the pot occasionally with a wet brush to prevent granulation around the pot. When the candy thermometer reaches 318° F, pour sugar over a lightly oiled marble slab. If various colors are desired, simply pour the sugar onto the slab in separate quantities and color as desired. At first the sugar will appear transparent.

After the sugar has been cooked and poured onto the marble slab, work it by turning the edges into the center from time to time to keep the edges as soft and as pliable as the center. When the sugar begins to hold its shape, pull several times until its texture is silky and shiny. If the sugar is pulled too much it will lose its gloss and get a waxy appearance. Place the sugar on a canvas in front of the batch warmer to keep it soft and pliable. The sugar is now ready to work with.

Fruit and Novelties

To make the pear tree shown in the photograph, the sugar was blown, much as a glass blower blows glass. A small round metal tube is inserted into a round ball of yellow-colored pulled sugar. Pull the sugar up and around the metal tube, then blow through the tube very gently so that the sugar will expand evenly. Pull the neck a little to form the elongated upper section. To keep the fragile sugar from breaking or cooling too fast, place your hands gently around it to keep it warm. After it is blown to the desired size or until it is quite thin, place the object in front of a cooling fan until it becomes firm; otherwise it will distort and collapse.

After the piece has been shaped and cooled, cut off the neck with a hot knife by cutting through the sugar next to the metal tube. Finish by placing a stem and leaf on top of the pear.

Color tone is applied by dipping a 1-inch brush into red paste coloring and brushing on the tone desired. This same procedure is used in making various fruits and vegetables, vases, etc., which are to be very thin and hollow inside.

A pear tree made of blown and pulled sugar.

A patriotic ribbon-and-bow design of
blown and pulled sugar.

Ribbons and Bows

Long strips of sugar are pulled for ribbons and bows. The width is determined by the size of the article or basket on which it is to be used. The sugar is pulled until it is very thin, making the width as uniform as possible. The sugar ribbon must not be pulled in a cool area; work only in front of the batch warmer.

To make bows, cut the ribbons into desired lengths. Bend the lengths so that the two ends meet with a loop between. Each bow or loop is made individually and is formed while the sugar is pliable enough to be shaped. The loops are stood up straight in front of the cooling fan on the marble slab so that they hold their shape. The loops needed, as well as the two long strips to be used as streamers, should all be made before putting them together.

To form the complete bow, take several loops and melt the cut edges over a bunsen burner; then attach each loop to form the bow.

Multicolored Ribbon

Color half of the sugar one color and leave the other half plain white. Pull the white sugar into a long but not too thin strip, and lay it in front of the batch warmer. Pull the colored sugar the same way and lay it so that the edge just covers the edge of the white strip. Press down on the two pieces of sugar so that they stick together, making one wide strip. Cut the strip in half again, and place one half so that it just overlaps the edge of the other half. This will make eight strips of alternating colors. This process may be repeated to make as many color strips as needed. Warm the strip evenly and then pull until the ribbon is long and thin. Place it on a canvas to cool and become firm. With a hot knife, heated over a flame, cut the strip into desired lengths. To reshape or bend, place the strip in front of the batch warmer to make it pliable before placing it on the article.

Pulled Sugar Basket Weaving

Basket weaving requires a board, either round or oval, which has an uneven number of holes drilled into the board at an angle (for instance, from 19 to 25 holes, but always an uneven number). Wooden or metal skewers, the desired height of the basket, are then placed into the holes. The board and skewers should be lightly greased.

The sugar is woven by pulling it into the shape of a cord and weaving it in and out of the skewers until the desired height is reached. At this point, the skewers are removed and replaced with skewers made from pulled sugar. The basket is finished with a double-twisted strand of pulled sugar around the top and bottom of the basket.

The handle is made by drawing a rather stiff piece of wire through a piece of pulled sugar. This action coats the wire, which may then be curved and shaped to form a handle of desired form. Attach handle to the basket and decorate as desired.

The finished products should be kept in an airtight container. By using silica gel (with indicator) or rock lime in the container, moisture will be kept to a minimum and the sugar work will be preserved.

CRYSTAL SUGAR

Crystal sugar work might be considered a preliminary lesson to pulled sugar work. Crystal sugar is less time consuming than pulled sugar; consequently, the finished product is ready faster and is of a durability that adapts to nut or candy dishes, floral baskets, etc.

Crystal sugar is cooked and prepared in the same way as pulled sugar. After cooking, it is poured onto a marble slab to form a round flat disc of the desired size. Allowed to cool sufficiently, it then is placed on a greased or lightly oiled inverted vase or bowl. Additional shaping around the bowl is necessary.

When the crystal sugar has cooled and set firmly, it is removed, set right side up, and finished with decorating touches using royal icing, pulled sugar flowers, or leaves. The result is a beautiful sugar piece which does not require the tedious work of the woven basket, etc., of the pulled sugar pieces.

A basket woven with pulled sugar.

GUM PASTE

Gum paste, or pastillage as it is sometimes called, is used for making model display pieces from skyscrapers to the smallest abode, and from simple baskets to the most intricate masterpieces. Gum paste is also excellent for making various flowers.

Before attempting to produce a showpiece of this kind, careful consideration should be given to plans, outlines, and photographic patterns.

Molding gum paste is easy if the mold is clean and dry and dusted lightly with cornstarch. It is wise to use a marble slab for rolling or cutting out the gum paste into various shapes; this will guarantee smooth pieces. Always be sure the slab is clean and free from dry pieces of gum paste before

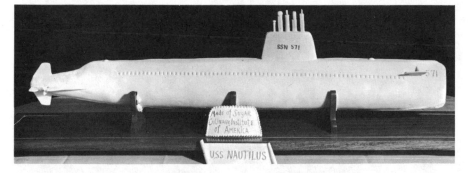

Above, model of the *U.S.S. Nautilus*, used as
a centerpiece. *Below*, model of a
stagecoach. Both models are made of gum paste.

using. The paste must also be worked smooth before rolling. Cutting should be done with a sharp knife or professional cutter. Always follow a pattern when cutting.

When molding gum paste, the mold should be lightly dusted first with cornstarch. Then the paste is forced into the mold, removed, and allowed to dry. The drying should be done at room temperature and on a hard, clean surface such as marble or glass. This enables the pieces to dry evenly. When these pieces are half dry, turn them over and allow the other side to dry. When they are completely dry on both sides, sand with a very fine sandpaper for added smoothness.

Now all the different pieces are ready to be assembled with the aid of additional gum paste that has been thinned down with water or egg white. Gum paste may be colored, but a plain white display piece seems more effective. If it is to be colored, however, only pastel shades should be used. When these sugar pieces are made for display purposes, the structure should be delicate—not too thick or heavy—as this detracts from their beauty.

There are several recipes for making gum paste. One of the most satisfactory, because of its simplicity and excellent results, follows.

GUM PASTE OR PASTILLAGE

Gelatin		1 oz
Water		8 oz (variable)
Confectioner's sugar	5 lb	

Method: Place gelatin in a container of water and heat until it is dissolved. Cool slightly, add the sugar, and mix until smooth. The consistency of the paste should be firm but pliable. Store it in a container until ready to work and roll. It may be stored in a refrigerator for further use.

NOUGAT CANDY FOR FANCY DISPLAY WORK

Nougat candy, used for display work, is quite simple to make. There are a variety of novelty pieces that may be made from it such as books, baskets, Easter eggs, hats, and so on. If it is possible to watch a demonstration, it will be easier for the beginner. After seeing an experienced worker handle the product, he should then practice doing it himself as much as possible.

A marble slab or a hard surface, which should be slightly oiled to prevent sticking, is required for this work. Other tools needed are a heavy rolling pin, spatula, and a French knife, slightly oiled.

When the candy is cooked, pour the mixture on the hard surface, turning the edges of the mixture toward the center until it starts to set. While it is still hot, cut out or mold the nougat into the shapes desired. It must be hot and flexible while handling. After it is cut or molded, allow it to cool and set until firm. If the mixture should cool and become firm while the cutting or molding is taking place, put it in a warm oven until it is flexible again.

For assembling the pieces, use a candy syrup of sugar and water cooked to 312°F. If a decoration of flowers or a special design is desired, royal icing may be used.

Nougat showpieces.

NOUGAT CANDY

Sugar	3 lb	
Water(1 pint)	1 lb	
Corn syrup		8 oz
Almonds, warm, sliced	3 lb	
	7 lb	8 oz

Method: Cook sugar, water, and syrup to 320°F. Add almonds and stir.

DECORATING WITH CHOCOLATE

Chocolate Molding or Couverture

Chocolate used for molding is called "Couverture" by European pastry chefs. It is manufactured in the United States in ten-pound blocks and can be purchased from any bakery supply house. Hershey's and Stollwerk's sweet chocolate are generally used for Couverture.

Chocolate used for molding or dipping should be melted gradually in a warm water bath or chocolate warmer until the temperature reaches approximately 86°F. The temperature is most important; if over- or underheated, the chocolate will turn gray and lose its gloss.

Break sweet chocolate into small pieces, and melt over a hot water bath (water temperature should not exceed 90°F), stirring well until all pieces are melted.

If chocolate is too thick, add melted cocoa butter until the proper running consistency is obtained. In extremely warm weather, a small addition of melted wax will definitely help the chocolate resist the heat: 1 ounce of melted wax to 1 pound of chocolate should be sufficient.

Pour about two-thirds of the whole quantity over a marble slab, and work it with a spatula or a scraper until cool. Mix with the remaining third, and melt to 84°-86°F. This process is called tempering.

Always use a wooden spoon or a steel spatula, rather than your hands, to work chocolate, because the temperature of your hands may cause the melted chocolate to discolor.

Chocolate molds are made out of tin or plastic and must always be kept dry and very clean. Scraping the inside of a mold with any sharp instrument will cause the chocolate to stick to the mold, so that future unmolding will be impossible.

CHOCOLATE DECORATIONS AND GARNISHES

The first step in making chocolate decorations is to cut a large bar of chocolate into small pieces with a French knife. The chocolate is then put into a bowl and melted at about 115°F. While the chocolate is melting it must be kept free from any contact with water or liquid of any kind as this tends to cause it to stiffen and lose its liquid form. Be careful not to overheat the chocolate or heat it too quickly. Temperatures over 120°F will make the chocolate thick and coarse.

Cool the chocolate to about 85°F; if necessary, "temper" or add some very finely grated chocolate, which will help the chocolate to set faster.

For curls or shavings, pour a small amount of chocolate on a marble slab and spread it with a spatula knife to form a strip about 4 inches wide and 1/8-inch thick. As soon as the chocolate begins to set, cut the shavings or curls with a quick, forward motion of the knife. The chocolate will curl as it comes off the knife in that shape.

For other decorations, let the chocolate cool and set, then cut it into squares or triangles with a knife, or into various shapes with assorted cutters. The chocolate may be stored in a cool, dry place until needed, and then easily be applied to finished pastries, cakes, and desserts. If your first attempt is not successful, nothing is lost. Simply scrape the chocolate back into the heating pot and start over from the beginning.

Chocolate for Piping or Decorating

Melt sweet chocolate in a cup, and add to it one-third of the same amount of fondant icing. Gradually add a little warm syrup or water to make a smooth piping consistency. Use while warm.

Chocolate Streusel Topping

This topping is widely used for finishing layer cakes and French pastries.

Gradually add a few drops of water to some melted sweet chocolate, and stir continually until chocolate thickens to a rather stiff consistency. Turn a sieve with a medium-sized mesh upside down, and press the chocolate through the sieve. Let the shredded chocolate hang until cool; then separate the shreds from the sieve, and keep in a cool place for future use.

Various Baking Temperatures
(Approximate Ranges)

Pan Breads	400°-425°F
Pan Rolls	400°F
Hearth Bread and Rolls	400°-425°F
Danish Pastry	375°-400°F
Various Sweet Doughs	375°-400°F
Coffee Cake	375°-400°F
Sheet Layer Cakes	375°F
Angel and Sponge Cake	350°-375°F
Heavy Fruit Cake	325°-350°F
Fruit and Soft Pies	375°F, 400°F, 425°F
Various Cookies	350°-375°F
Puffs and Eclairs	375°-400°F
Various Muffins	400°-425°F
Puff Pastes	350°-375°F
Baked Puddings	350°-375°F

Bakers' Dictionary

Ash: The powdery, incombustible residue left after burning matter.

Average flour value: Value composed of four factors: color of flour, loaves per barrel, size of loaf, and quality of bread as applied to any given shipment of flour.

Baba au Rhum: French sweet-dough cake soaked with rum.

Bacteria: Numerous microscopic organisms, various species of which are concerned in fermentation and spoilage.

Bain Marie: A double boiler, or open vessel, which has a loose bottom for the reception of hot water, and is used to keep sauces at boiling point.

Bake: To cook by dry heat in a closed place, as an oven.

Baked Alaska: Cake layer topped with firm ice cream, completely covered with meringue, then delicately browned in a very hot oven.

Baking or Bicarbonate of Soda: A sodium salt of carbonic acid having the ability to combine with acid to produce carbon dioxide. It is alkaline in nature.

Baking Powder: A chemical leavening agent composed of baking soda, dry acid, and, usually, cornstarch to absorb air moisture; when wet, carbon dioxide (a gas) is given off to raise the batter.

Barrel: A flat ended, wooden, somewhat cylindrical container with bulging sides. The measure of what a standard size barrel contains, as 31½ gallons of liquid or 196 lbs of flour.

Bars: Cookies made in oblong shapes.

Batter: A pourable mixture of combined ingredients such as flour, sugar, eggs, shortening, milk, etc.

Biscuit: Small roll made with yeast dough. Small round bread stuff made of dough raised with baking powder. Kind of crisp or hard bread, thin and flat, made without leavening.

Biscuit Tortoni: Mousse, containing and sprinkled with macaroon crumbs, frozen in individual paper cases.

Blanch: To remove the skins from various nuts, etc., by scalding.

Blancmange: Molded white pudding of milk, sugar, and cornstarch, or gelatin.

Bleeding: Term applied to dough that has been cut and left unsealed at the cut, thus permitting the escape of air and gas.

Blend: A mixture of two or more flavorings or grades of flour.

Boil: To bubble, emitting vapor, when heat is applied. Boiling temperature for water is considered as $212°F$ at ordinary altitudes, but varies with other liquids and other altitudes.

Boiled icing: Made by boiling sugar and water to thread stage $(238°F)$, then adding it to beaten egg whites and confectioner's sugar.

Bolting: Sifting of ground grain to remove the bran.

Boston Brown Bread: A dark, sweet bread (not yeast raised) containing among the ingredients cornmeal and molasses, steamed and not baked.

Boston cream pie: Plain or sponge-cake layers filled with cream filling, often topped with confectioner's sugar or thin chocolate frosting.

Bouchées: Very small puff paste patties, small enough to be a mouthful only.

Bowl knife: A spatula or flexible dull-edged knife used to scrape batter or dough from bowl sides.

Bran: Skin or outer covering of the wheat berry removed during milling.

Bran muffin: Sweet muffin containing a large percentage of bran.

Brandy: An alcoholic liquor distilled from fermented fruit juice or wine.

Bread: The accepted term for food of flour, sugar, shortening, salt, and liquid made light by the action of yeast.

Bread dough: The uncooked mass of ingredients used to make bread.

Bread faults: Deviations from standards of perfection, used to determine wrong factors in the process of production of bread.

Bread schedule: List of exact periods of dough fermentation; also shows time needed for completing the baking process.

Bread scoring: Analysis of finished loaf to determine quality.

Bread shop order: Form sent to shop foreman giving amount of bread needed for production during, or by, a given time.

Brioche: A light sweet dough, baked in large or small moulds.

Buns: Small cakes of bread dough, sometimes slightly sweetened or flavored.

Butter: Fat obtained by churning sweet or sour cream.

Butter cream frosting: Rich, uncooked frosting containing powdered sugar, butter and/or other shortening, and egg white.

Butter horns: Basic sweet dough cut and shaped like horns.

Butter sponge: Sponge cake batter, to which shortening is added. Used for Torten and French pastry, also some layers.

Butterscotch: A flavor produced by the use of butter and brown sugar.

Butter stars: Cookies made by pressing rich dough through star tube.

Cacao: An evergreen tree, native to tropical America, from which chocolate is obtained.

Cake: A leavened and shortened sweet product containing flour, sugar, salt, egg, milk, liquid, flavoring, shortening, and leavening agent.

Cake faults: Deviations from standards of perfection for the type.

Cake machine: Machine with vertical agitators operating at different speeds, used for mixing cake ingredients.

Cane sugar: A sweet carbohydrate obtained from sugar cane.

Caramel buns: Sweet dough pieces baked in a sugared pan.

Caramel icing: Cooked icing of brown sugar, shortening, and milk.

Caramel sugar: Cane sugar boiled to a certain density, then cooled and pulled for use in decorating.

Caramelized sugar: Dry sugar heated, with constant stirring, until it melts and darkens in color; used for flavoring and color.

Caraway seeds: Aromatic seeds, tiny and egg-shaped. Used in sauerkraut, cookies, cheese, German rye bread.

Carbohydrates: Sugars and starches derived chiefly from vegetable sources, which contained set amounts of carbon, hydrogen, and oxygen according to the kind of carbohydrate.

Carbon dioxide: A colorless, tasteless, edible gas obtained during fermentation or from the combination of soda and acid.

Carbonated ammonia: Leavening agent made of ammonia and carbonic acid.

Cardamon: Angular, aromatic seeds of herb grown in India and Ceylon, and having aniselike taste. Used whole or ground in pickling, breads, cookies, and many Scandinavian desserts.

Casein: The principal nitrogenous, or protein, part of milk.

Chafing dish: A dish (usually silver) set within another dish containing hot water, with a small lamp underneath, and used for keeping foods hot until served.

Charlotte: Mold lined with ladyfingers and filled with fruit and whipped cream. **Russe:** Mold lined with ladyfingers and filled with Bavarian cream.

Cheese cake: Cake made of sweet or short dough base with a filling of cheese combined with eggs and milk.

Cheese torte: A rich cheese mixture baked in a shell of combined crumbs, sugar, and butter.

Cherries jubilee: Cherries set aflame with Kirsch or brandy. Often served over vanilla ice cream.

Chocolate snaps: Fairly crisp drop cookies flavored with chocolate.

Chou pâté: Paste used in making eclairs, cream puffs, French doughnuts, etc.

Cinnamon: The aromatic bark of certain trees of the laurel family; ground and used as a spice flavoring.

Citron: The sweetened rind of a fruit.

Clear flour: Flour made from middlings after patent flour is taken.

Cobbler: Sweetened fruit in deep dish, topped with upper crust and baked.

Cocoa: A powder made from chocolate minus most of its cocoa butter.

Coconut: The inside meat of the coconut, shredded or grated.

Coffee cake: Sweet bread in various shapes, with filling and topping.

Colors: Shades produced by using vegetable dyes; flour colors.

Compôte: Fruit stewed in syrup, or a mixture of different stewed fruits.

Compounds: In the baking industry, certain mixtures of fats and oils.

Congealing point: Temperature at which a liquid becomes solid.

Corn flour: Coarse flour ground from corn; finer than meal.

Cornmeal: Granular form of corn somewhat coarser than corn flour.

Corn muffin: Sweet muffin containing corn flour or meal.

Cornet: A cornucopia-shaped (horn-shaped) container of paper or cloth used for tubing soft doughs, frostings, etc.

Cottage cheese: The drained curd of soured cow's milk.

Coupe: A dessert served in a champagne glass, and usually made of fresh fruit and ice cream.

Cream: The fat part of cow's milk; a thickened, cooked mass of sugar, egg, milk, and a thickener; used for pies and fillings.

Cream cheese: The drained curd of soured cream, pressed.

Cream pies: One-crust pies having cream filling, topped with whipped cream or meringue.

Cream puffs: Baked puffs of cream puff dough (chou pâté) which are hollow; usually filled with whipped cream or a cream filling.

Cream rolls: Puff paste rolled and baked in spiral shape, then filled with whipped cream or marshmallow.

Creaming: The process of beating sugar and shortening.

Crème: Cream or cream sauce.

Crème Chantilly: Cream whipped with vanilla and sugar.

Creme de Menthe: A green flavoring of light mint taste.

Crepes: Very thin pancakes. Suzette: Pancakes served in butter sauce flavored with orange, lemon, curaçao; flamed in brandy.

Crescent rolls: Hard-crusted rolls shaped into crescents, often with seeds on top.

Croissant: Rich crescent-shaped French roll usually served at breakfast.

Crullers: Long, twisted baking powder doughnuts.

Culinary: This word is applied to anything connected with the art of cooking or baking.

Cupcakes: Small cakes of layer cake batter baked in muffin pans.

Currant: The acidulous berry of a shrub; usually used dried.

Custard: A sweetened mixture of eggs and milk which is baked or cooked over hot water.

Danish pastry: A flaky yeast dough having butter rolled into it and filled with almond, cheese, jam, or other filling.

Date: The fruit of a species of palm, very sweet.

Date filling: A cooked blend of dates, water, and sugar.

Decoration: Trimming with fancy designs or ornamentation.

Detection of flour: The manner in which poor flour is contrasted with a good flour to show that the former has been bleached.

Determination of ash: The finding of the ash content of flour.

Determination of flour color: Comparison of flour samples to show how they approach color standards.

Dextrin: A soluble, gummy substance formed from starch by the action of heat, ferments, etc., having characteristic properties.

Dextrose: Sugar of vegetables (except beet) less sweet than cane or beet sugar and more simple in structure, chemically speaking.

Diastase: An enzyme possessing the power to convert starches into dextrin and maltose (a simple sugar).

Dissolve: To liquefy or carry in suspension in liquid.

Divider: A machine to cut dough automatically into a required size.

Dough: The thick, uncooked mass of combined ingredients for bread, rolls, cookies, etc.; usually applied to bread.

Dough room: Special room in which bread doughs are mixed.

Dough room record: A sheet of paper showing the time and losses of dough going through different stages (bread dough).

Dough sheet: A paper showing the formulas for a day's doughs.

Dough temperature: Temperature of dough at different stages.

Dough time cards: Cards usually punched with a time clock at different stages of dough processing.

Doughnut: A round cake, usually with center hole, made of yeast or baking powder dough and cooked in hot deep fat.

Doughnut kettle: A large kettle used for frying doughnuts.

Doughnut screens: Screens used to lift doughnuts from fat or for keeping them under the fat surface during cooking.

Doughnut sticks: Wooden sticks for turning doughnuts while cooking.

Drops: Small globules of liquid that will drip instead of flow from spoon or container; a form of cookie.

Dry fruit: Fruit from which moisture has been removed by drying.

Dry milk: Milk from which water has been removed by drying.

Dry yeast: A dehydrated form of yeast.

Dusting: Distributing a film of flour on pans or work bench.

Dusting flour: Flour spread on work bench to prevent sticking.

Eclair: A long, thin shell of the same paste as cream puffs.

Egg wash: A mixture of eggs and water (or milk) in equal parts applied to an unbaked product by brush to produce a glazed effect and to give the product a rich brown color.

Emulsify: To combine ingredients together such as water and fat.

English brandy snaps: Spicy cookies, very small and flat.

Enriched bread: Bread made from enriched flour or containing federally prescribed amounts of thiamin, riboflavin, iron, and niacin.

Enzyme: A minute substance produced by living organisms which has the power to bring about changes in organic materials.

Evaporated milk: Unsweetened canned milk from which water has been removed before canning.

Expansion of dough: The stage of dough production where the most air has been assimilated.

Extract: Essence of fruits or spices used as flavoring.

Ferment: A substance, such as yeast, producing fermentation.

Fermentation: The chemical changes of an organic compound due to action of living organisms, as yeast, producing the formation of the leavening gas, carbon dioxide.

Fig: A pear-shaped fruit of the fig tree.

Filberts: Cultivated hazelnuts.

Filbert rolls: Jelly-roll type cake with roasted filberts in filling and batter.

Fillings: Sweet creams, jams, etc., baked between baked layers, in cake rolls, or shaped into yeast-raised goods.

Finger roll: A bun about three inches long and one inch wide.

Firing: Process of heating an oven with fuel.

Flambé: Dessert over which spirits are poured and lighted.

Flavor: An extract, emulsion, or spice used to produce a pleasant taste. The taste of a finished product.

Fleurons: Garnitures made from light puff paste cut into oval, diamond, or crescent shapes, and served with meat, fish, or soup.

Flour: Finely ground meal of grain (wheat, rye, etc.).

Flour scales: Large platform scales used to show weight of flour when delivered and when used, to detect losses by shrinkage.

Fluff: A mass of beaten egg white and crushed fruit.

Foam: Mass of beaten egg and sugar, as in sponge cake, before adding flour.

Fold: The method of lapping dough over on itself after it reaches right fermentation, as in making yeast-raised sweet goods.

Fondant: An icing of boiled sugar and water, without egg white.

Fondant slab: Marble slab on which fondant is worked until creamy.

Formula: In baking, a recipe giving ingredients, amounts to be used, and method of combining them.

Foundation: The reinforced base on which an oven or machine rests.

French bread: An unsweetened crusty bread baked in a narrow strip and containing very little shortening.

French doughnuts: Doughnuts made of chou pâté.

French knife: A long knife with pointed blade used in cutting cakes, doughs, and nuts.

Fritters: Doughnuts made from cream puff paste and fried in hot deep fat. Fruit-filled drops of heavy cake batter fried in deep fat.

Fruit cake: A cake containing large amounts of dried fruits and nuts with only enough batter to bind the fruit together.

Frying: In the baking industry, cooking in hot deep fat.

Fuel: Anything which is burned to give heat.

Garnishing bag: Similar to a cornet and equipped with fancy tips.

Gâteau: French term for cake.

Gelatinization of starch: Formation of jellylike substance when moistened starch is cooked.

Germ: That part of seed (such as in grain) from which the new plant grows.

Ginger: The spicy root of a tropical plant used for flavoring.

Glacé: Sugar treated so as to look like ice.

Gliadin: The part of gluten that gives it elasticity.

Glucose: A simple sugar made by action of acid on starch (corn syrup).

Gluten: The protein part of flour which gives structure to bakery products by enabling flour to expand around air or gas and to hold the texture so formed. The determining quality factor.

Glutenin: The part of gluten which gives it strength.

Gourmet: A connoisseur of fine foods.

Grading: Separating middlings of wheat according to size.

Graham flour: Unbolted wheat meal.

Graham muffin: A sweet muffin with graham flour as its main ingredient.

Greasing: Spreading a film of fat on a surface.

Gum Arabic: A gum obtained from a species of acacia tree.

Gum paste: A white modeling substance of gum tragacanth or gelatin, water, and sugar.

Gum tragacanth: A gum used to give firmness.

Hamburger roll: A soft round bun about four inches in diameter.

Hardness of water: An indication of mineral salts in greater amount than is found in soft water.

Hazelnut: Nut of a wild American shrub, smaller than the filbert.

Hearth: The heated baking surface or floor of an oven.

Holland rusk: Toast of yeast biscuits rich in milk, eggs, etc.

Homemade bread: Plain topped bread rolled in flour before panning, or that baked in household-type bread pans.

Honey: A sweet syrup substance made by bees from flower nectar.

Horn of plenty: Cornucopia-shaped cookie made with gum paste, butter cream trimming, or bread dough.

Horseshoes: Danish or puff pastry shaped like horseshoes.

Hot-cross buns: Sweet, yeast-raised buns with raisins added, marked on top with a cross in dough or a frosted cross. Lenten favorite.

Humidity: Amount of moisture in the air.

Hydrogenated oil: Oil treated with hydrogen to give a type of shortening.

Hygrometer: An instrument to determine the degree of humidity.

Ice: To frost or put on an icing or frosting; frozen water.

Icing: A frosting or coating for cakes made by mixing confectioner's sugar with water, egg whites, etc.

Infection: The presence of injurious microorganisms.

Ingredients: Food materials blended to give palatable products.

Inventory: Itemized list of goods and equipment on hand, together with the estimated worth or cost.

Invert sugar: A simple sugar; combination of dextrose and levulose.

Jelly: A stiffened combination of fruit juice and sugar, stiffened by the action of the sugar on the pectin in the fruit.

Jelly wreath: A rolled ring of basic sweet dough containing jelly.

Kernel paste: A mass of ground apricot kernels and sugar.

Kisses: A meringue confection of egg white and sugar baked slowly.

Lactose: The sugar of cow's milk.

Lady Baltimore cake: Rich white layer cake with fruit and nut filling and white icing.

Lard: Rendered hog fat.

Leavening: Raising or lightening by air, steam, or gas (carbon dioxide).

Leavening agent: An ingredient (or ingredients) used to introduce carbon dioxide: yeast, baking powder, or soda plus sour milk.

Leipziger stollen: Very rich coffee cake with a great deal of fruit.

Levulose: A simple sugar found in honey and fruits.

Line: To place paste, pie crust, ladyfingers, etc., around the inside edge or bottom of moulds, rings, plates.

Linzer torte: A heavy cake of macaroon paste and jelly.

Loaf bread: Bread baked in pans.

Loaf cake: Cake baked in a bread pan or similar deep container.

Macaroon paste: A combination of almond and kernel paste.

Macaroons: Small cookies of nut paste (as almond), sugar, and egg white.

Make up: Method of mixing ingredients or handling of dough.

Malt extract: A syrupy liquid obtained from malt mash.

Maple flavoring: An extract of maple sugar or a syrup so flavored.

Maraschino: Cordial distilled from Maraca cherry juice.

Maraschino cherries: Artificially colored white cherries in maraschino.

Marble cake: Cake of two or three colored batters partially mixed.

Marrons: Chestnuts. **Glacés:** Chestnuts preserved in syrup or candied, used in making fancy desserts.

Marshmallow: A white confection of meringuelike consistency.

Marzipan: Almond paste used for modeling, masking, and torten.

Masking: Act of covering with icing or frosting or such.

Meal: Coarsely ground grain; unbolted wheat flour.

Measuring: Apportioning ingredients by area, volume, or weight. Ascertaining dimensions, capacities, or weight.

Measuring cup: A standardized cup marked with fractions of a cup, used for accurate measure.

Measuring spoons: Sets of standardized spoons (tablespoon, teaspoon, half and quarter) ensuring accurate measurement.

Melba sauce: Raspberry and currant jelly made into a sauce.

Melba toast: Thin slices of bread toasted to a pleasing crispness and golden color.

Melting point: The temperature at which a solid becomes liquid.

Meringue: A white frothy mass of beaten egg white and sugar.

Metric system: A system of weights and measures based on multiple units of ten; used in the baking industry chiefly for flour analysis.

Middlings: Coarse particles of ground wheat made during rolling of the grain in flour mills.

Milk bread: White bread in which all liquid is milk or which contains not less than 8.8 parts (by weight) of milk solids for each 100 parts of flour (by weight). This is a federal standard that is rigidly enforced.

Milk solids: All of cow's milk except the water.

Mincemeat: Combination filling of fruit, spices, beef, and suet.

Mix: The combined ingredients of a batter or dough.

Mixing: The blending of ingredients.

Mixing bowl: A concave, hemispherical container for mixing.

Mocha: A flavor combination of coffee and cocoa.

Moisture: Water held in or appearing on a substance.

Molasses: Light to dark brown syrup obtained in making cane sugar.

Mold infection: Deleterious microscopic organisms of vegetable nature.

Molder: Machine that shapes dough pieces for various shapes.

Mousse: A light, frozen dessert consisting of whipped cream, pâté-a-bombé, and flavoring.

Muffins: Small, light quickbread baked in muffin pans.

Mushrooms: Schaum torte confections in mushroom shapes.

Napoleons: Delicate French pastry made with puff paste in layers with a cream filling between and thin frosting or powdered sugar on top.

Neapolitan ice cream: Layered brick ice cream in different flavors.

Nesselrode pie: Rum-flavored Bavarian cream pie filling with mixed preserved fruits and chestnuts added in a flaky pie shell and topped with shaved chocolate.

Nougat: A confection made from almonds, pistachio nuts, and sugar.

Oatmeal: Meal made by grinding oats.

One mix: A cake mixing method where all ingredients are combined and beaten at one time.

Pandowdy: Sweetened and spiced sliced applies covered with a rich baking powder biscuit dough, then baked. Served hot with cream.

Pans (tins): Variously shaped metal containers for cooking and baking.

Parker House rolls: Folded buns of fairly rich dough.

Pastillage: A gum paste used in making candies, fancy pieces, flowers, etc.

Patent flour: The fine meal of ground spring wheat.

Pectin: A natural fruit substance which, when in right balance with sugar and acid, forms fruit juice into a jelly.

Petit fours: Small cakes of various shapes and flavors.

Pfeffernusse: Christmas cookie, spicy and hard.

Philadelphia cinnamon bun: Raisin-filled cinnamon bun with luscious sticky topping.

Pie: Dessert with pastry bottom, fruit or cream filling, and meringue, whipped cream, or pastry top.

Pignoli: Pine nuts.

Pine nuts: Small sweet seeds contained in cones of certain pine trees, usually roasted or salted.

Plain tube decorating: Decorations made with plain round tube.

Poppy seeds: Fragrant seeds from Holland, used in breads, rolls, noodles, etc.

Profiteroles: Small cream puffs filled with cream and covered with a sauce. They are sometimes made very small and served with soup.

Proof box: Box or cabinet equipped with shelves; it also permits the introduction of heat and steam; used for fermenting dough.

Proofing period: The time during which dough rises.

Puff paste: Rich pastry with rolled butter and special shortening for added flakiness.

Pumpernickel: Coarse, somewhat acid rye bread.

Pumpernickel meal: Coarse rye flour.

Punch: See **Fold.**

Quiche Lorraine: Open-faced cheese pie with diced ham or bacon added.

Quick bread: Dough for bread or rolls raised by baking powder.

Raisins: Dried sweet grapes, either dark or bleached.

Rock sugar: A candy preparation used in the construction of fancy pieces.

Rocks: Small rough-surfaced cookies resembling stone shapes.

Rolling pin: Smooth-surfaced wooden piece for rolling dough.

Rolls: Soft breads sometimes called buns; hard-crusted pieces of lean dough.

Rope: A spoiling bacterial growth in bread formed during production.

Rounding: Shaping of dough pieces to seal ends and prevent bleeding.

Royal icing: Decorative frosting of cooked sugar and egg whites.

Sabayon: Pudding sauce, made in double boiler, of eggs, sugar, and wine. Served hot.

Sally Lunn: Southern bread sometimes yeast-leavened and baked in tube pan. Or it may be made with baking powder and baked in round cake or pie pans.

Salt: Sodium chloride; used for flavor and dough control.

Saturation: Absorption to the limit of capacity.

Scale: An instrument for weighing.

Scaling: Apportioning batter or dough according to unit weight.

Schedule: Shop form designating amount and types of goods to be made and hour when needed.

Scone: Typical Scottish hot bread or cake baked on a griddle or in the oven.

Score: To score is to make incisions forming a pattern on cakes or pies, etc.

Scoring: Judging finished goods according to points of favor.

Sesame seed: Seed imported from Asia. Creamy white, tiny, somewhat slippery to touch, with faint nutty odor and nutlike flavor. Nice in breads, cookies, etc.

Shoo Fly pie: Brown sugar and

molasses-flavored cake, baked in a pie shell.

Short pastry: A dough made with a high fat content, such as pie crust.

Shortbread: Crisp cookie, rich in butter or other shortening, of Scottish origin.

Shortening: Fat or oil used to tenderize flour products.

Shrink: To shrink is to roll out paste and allow it to rest before baking in order to prevent shrinkage.

Sifting: Passing through fine sieve for perfect blending and to remove foreign or oversize particles.

Snaps: Small cookies that run flat during baking.

Solidifying point: Temperature at which a fluid changes to a solid.

Soufflé: Baked dish made basically of milk and eggs, to which the beaten egg whites, folded in last, give a high, puffed, airy lightness; may be main dish or dessert.

Spices: Aromatic vegetable substances (dry) for flavoring.

Spoon bread: Southern corn bread made in a casserole, so delicate it must be served with a spoon.

Springerle: Traditional German cookie, anise-flavored, with a raised design on top.

Stollen: Raisin-filled rich yeast bread.

Strawberries Romanoff: Fine, ripe strawberries marinated in Cointreau or Kirsch, with whipped cream folded in or used as topping.

Straight flour: Flour containing all of the wheat berry except the bran and feeds; termed 100 percent extraction flour.

Strudel: Rich pastry filled with apples, cherries, plums, etc.

Tarts: Pastries with heavy fruit or cream filling.

Tea rolls: Small sweet buns.

Temperature: Degree of heat or cold.

Tempering: Adjusting temperature of ingredients to a certain degree.

Testing: Trying a cake or bread at the oven for doneness; checking product or ingredients for quality, according to a set method.

Texture: Interior grain or structure of a baked product as shown by a cut surface; the feeling of a substance under the fingers.

Thermometer: An instrument for measuring temperature.

Torten: Large fancy cakes enriched with creams, marzipan, etc.

Trifle: Dessert of English origin made of layers of wine-sprinkled spongecake slices, custard sauce or whipped cream, and preserves or jelly.

Troughs: Large, rather shallow containers, usually on wheels, used for holding large masses of rising dough.

Tubing: Pressing a substance through a decorating or other tube.

Turn: When puff paste is mixed,

rolled out, folded over one third, and then the other third is folded over this, this operation is called giving one turn.

Tutti frutti: A confection or filling made of a fruit mixture.

Vanilla bean: Dried bean of a tropical orchid, used for flavoring. Extract is delightful in desserts, cakes, cookies, etc.

Vegetable colors: Vegetable liquids or paste, used for coloring.

Vienna bread: A hearth bread with heavy, crisp crust, sometimes finished with a seed topping.

Vol-au-Vent: A light puff paste, cut either round or oval, and usually filled with meat or fish.

Wash: A liquid brushed on the surface of an unbaked product (may be water, milk, starch solution, thin syrup, or egg).

Washington pie: Spongecake layers filled with jelly, sprinkled on top with confectioner's sugar.

Whip: To beat to a froth; an instrument consisting of strong wires held together by a handle and used for whipping.

Whole wheat: Unbolted wheat meal.

Yeast: A microscopic fungus (plant) which reproduces by budding and causes fermentation and the giving off of carbon dioxide.

Zwieback: A toast made of rich coffee cake.

Index